ernstfried prade

windsurfing

ep sport

About the Author :

Ernstfried Prade (born in 1945) is an experienced graphic designer and boat designer. He was one of the first in Europe to practise windsurfing. In 1973 he was second in the European championships and in 1973 and 1974 he was the West German windsurfing champion. He is an instructor of the Association of German Windsurfing Schools and can therefore share his wide sailing experience and expert theoretical knowledge with his pupils. He has had many articles published and is editor of the magazine 'Windsurfing'. His involvement in many different areas of the sport has given him the best possible experience on which to draw in this comprehensive book on windsurfing. Ernstfried Prade's first book *Windsurfing – den Wind in den Händen (Windsurfing – The Wind In Your Hands –* Bussesche Verlagshandlung, Herford) was published in 1975.

Acknowledgements for the English Edition :

Translation: Wendy Gill
Editing: Susan Joslin

The publishers would particularly like to thank Brian Johnson, founder of the UK Windsurfing Association, for his help in ensuring that this translation meets as closely as possible the terminology and conditions of the sport in the United Kingdom and the Commonwealth.

ISBN 0 7158 06351

Published by EP Publishing Ltd, East Ardsley, Wakefield, West Yorkshire, 1979

Text set in 10/12 pt Monophoto Univers, printed by photo-lithography, and bound in Great Britain by G. Beard & Son Ltd, Brighton

Illustration credits :

Werkfoto G. Bourguignon, p.20
N. Darby, p.7
R. Denk, p.35
Werkfoto Eckel, p.20
M. Garff, p.66
H. Hamm, p.6
J. Kemmler, pp.2/3, 8, 21, 28, 29, 36, 37, 38, 39, 41, 42, 45, 48, 49, 50, 51, 53, 54, 62, 63, 64, 70, 76, 79, 81, 82, 83, 84, 85, 86, 87, 88, 89, 90, 91, 94, 95, 115, 128
E. Prade, pp.4, 8, 9, 14, 16, 17, 19, 20, 32, 33, 34, 66, 67, 69, 72, 73, 74, 75, 95, 98, 99, 103, 113, 119, 120, 122, 123, 124, 125, 126, 127, 129
U. Seer, pp.132, 133
P. Stückl, pp.24, 52, 55, 56, 57, 58, 97, 98, 99, 100, 104, 109, 110, 116, 129, 134
J. Stuwe, p.138
H. Taubinger, pp.130, 131
Windsurfing Deutschland, p.23

Contents

Introduction

Sailing – Surfing – Windsurfing

Since time immemorial men have used the power of the wind to propel sailed vessels across the water, the principle of steering and propulsion remaining unchanged. However, with the new sport of windsurfing a different form of steering has come into being – a way of steering without a rudder. A windsurfer steers his course by means of his sail and the position of his feet.

Indians on the Amazon

It is not clear who first had the idea of mounting a moveable rig on a floating body.

It is possible that the Indians were the first to use a boat without a rudder. Their raft-like boats were steered by inclining the mast. Since they did not use this form of sailing as a sport, and therefore found it too tedious to hold constantly on to the mast, they positioned the mast in a board with several holes. Whenever they wanted to change direction they lifted the mast out of its hole and repositioned it in a different hole. By this method the sail could be moved to leeward or windward

and also fore and aft. It is not known if the sail was attached only to a wishbone boom, as in windsurfing today, or whether it was also held by a main sheet.

Newman Darby's Sailboard

Newman Darby invented a steerable and extremely useful sailboard in 1964. In shape, however, the boat bore more resemblance to a sailing boat than to a surfboard. Newman Darby used a square sail placed on one corner, fastened at the top and bottom to the mast and at the sides to a stay gaff. The entire rig was moveable by means of a rope but was permanently attached to the boat. Newman Darby stood on his boat in front of the sail and leaned his body against the wind pressure. He steered by inclining the sail fore and aft.

Hawaii – Sailing with Rainer Schwarz

In 1966 Rainer Schwarz from Munich patented a sailing vessel and a new steering principle. His discovery was a kind of paddle-boat on which he sat, holding on to two poles joined together at the bottom, between which the sail was stretched. He

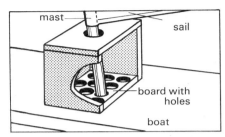

The first steerable sailing vessel without a rudder – it has a board with several holes to hold the mast in different positions

1964 – Newman Darby sailing his craft standing to leeward

could steer by means of the free-moving sail. This craft, however, was never put into production since its inventor himself soon discovered that holding and steering this form of rig was much too tiring and laborious.

Hoyle Schweitzer and the Windsurfer

It was Hoyle Schweitzer and Jimmy Drake, two sportsmen from California, who finally put windsurfing on its feet. Hoyle Schweitzer laid the foundations of windsurfing by placing the emphasis on 'surfing'. He and his colleague Drake had been keen surfers on the Californian coast for many years. When the waves were small and yet there was a strong wind they had the idea of making use of their surfboards by somehow propelling them by wind rather than by wave.

At first Hoyle Schweitzer experimented with a simple piece of sailcloth which he held in his hands. He gradually refined his basic idea until the modern windsurfer came into existence. We do not know if it was Newman Darby's craft or some other that was his first inspiration. However, it is certain that with unflagging energy he promoted windsurfing throughout the world and can therefore be called the father of the sport.

After Hoyle Schweitzer had perfected his original windsurfer in 1969 – it consisted of a normal surfboard, as used in the huge waves of Hawaii, and a triangular sail fastened to a mast and

Hoyle Schweitzer, the father of windsurfing, is also an enthusiastic surfer

Schweitzer's original windsurfer. Construction and materials have remained unchanged since 1969

stretched by means of a wishbone shaped boom – there was a worldwide interest in the further development of this craft. After very few years there were twenty different versions on the market, basically all copies of the original. Windsurfing is regarded by the experts as the greatest development in sailing for many years. For many enthusiasts it means the direct confrontation of man with wind and waves. For families on holiday, or for businessmen sitting at their desks all day and wanting some form of exercise and relaxation, windsurfing is the ideal sport. With correct instruction it can be learnt in a few hours.

This book is for all who wish to learn this wonderful sport quickly and easily and it also includes, for the expert windsurfer, a whole range of new ideas, new techniques and useful tips which will help him get the very best out of his sport.

Note: Windsurfing should never be carried out where it is dangerous or likely to cause annoyance to other people, such as in bathing areas or entrances to harbours.

Equipment

The Board

As has already been mentioned in the introduction, windsurfing is derived from surfing. Some boards, like Hoyle Schweitzer's original board, are identical to ordinary surfboards. Today surfers are using somewhat shorter boards (1.8 m) but experts still recommend the use of the long boards measuring up to 3 m for the huge waves found in Hawaii and Australia. Windsurfing boards are mostly between 3.5 m and 4 m long and 60–70 cm wide. The volume is about 180–250 l capacity and they weigh anything between 12 kg and 25 kg. Depending, of course, on the construction and the material used, they can be flexible, adapting to the waves, or rigid, ploughing through the water.

Non-Slip Standing Surface

Some boards appear to be beautifully constructed yet their performance is very poor. The most important quality of a windsurfing board, for beginners and experts alike, is the non-slip surface. Windsurfing is a sport where a lot of movement is required and therefore in order that all movements may be carried out safely and freely it is absolutely essential that the board's upper surface is non-slip. Some boards have a standing surface in the centre only, the rest of the surface having a high gloss polyester finish. It would be impossible to get full enjoyment from windsurfing on one of these boards since as soon as you tried out a new step you would simply slip off! The whole surface of the board should be non-slip. Unfortunately, some manufacturers have gone too far the other way. Those surfers who have taken to the water with their board in the summer with bare knees – and surfing is a summer sport – and have fallen on a rough hard polyester surface and grazed their knees badly will appreciate that the standing surface should be non-slip but not too rough. There are a few do-it-yourself tips:

- Smooth polyester boards can be rubbed down with emery paper.
- Home-made boards can be given a final lacquer and then waxed. Wax is an excellent means of giving any board a non-slip surface. The only disadvantage is that the board is sometimes marked.
- A short-term answer, for racing for example, is to apply adhesive tape with a sticky upper surface.

Eight boards – note the differences

The Shape of the Board

There are many opinions as to which is the best shape of board. The main consideration must be the performance requirements of the board in use. A high-speed windsurfer, which is usually long and narrow, has a different function from a universal board, which is stable and buoyant in the water. Hoyle Schweitzer's original board can be seen as the happy medium. Its biggest disadvantage is that it is not suitable for heavy surfers. It is important not to regard the board as a kind of balance beam; keeping your balance at all costs must not take precedence over your enjoyment of the sport! Therefore, boards narrower than 50 cm are really only for the experts, who for the sake of adding one or two knots to their speed must constantly be on the alert against toppling over. The board must be examined closely. For example, has it any sharp edges? Those who have ventured into high waves with a rigid polyester board will know the value of flexible boards with rubber edges. Windsurfing can be compared with skiing, where flexible skis are much more useful on bumpy slopes and rigid skis are used for downhill racing. So, too, in windsurfing flexible boards behave better in the waves while high-speed boards should be rigid.

In this connection the fin or skeg must be mentioned. When you are carrying the board on land or if you capsize in the water, there is always the danger of the fin breaking if it is too pointed or too rigid.

The Daggerboard Case

The most critical point on any board is the daggerboard case; it is always endangered whenever the daggerboard runs aground. Latest developments in design have taken this disadvantage into account and have incorporated daggerboards which retract or fold back on impact. When buying a board it is always advisable to have a good look at the daggerboard case as it is here that good or shoddy workmanship can most easily be seen. The daggerboard must sit well in the case without much play and you should be able to lift it up without pulling and pushing. When you replace it, it must slide down without rubbing unduly against the walls of the case as this could damage it.

▶

A windsurfer, with its few individual parts, can be assembled in minutes. This is the biggest advantage of this uncomplicated sport

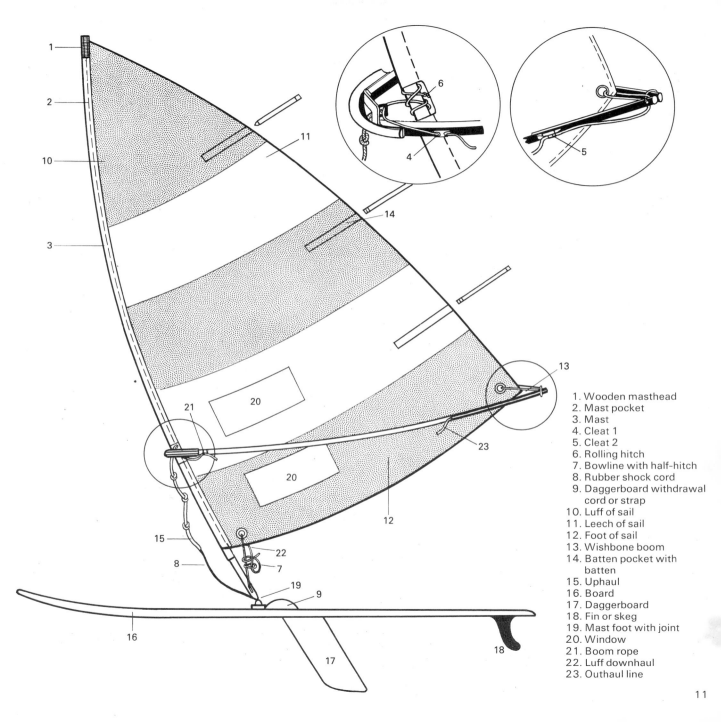

1. Wooden masthead
2. Mast pocket
3. Mast
4. Cleat 1
5. Cleat 2
6. Rolling hitch
7. Bowline with half-hitch
8. Rubber shock cord
9. Daggerboard withdrawal cord or strap
10. Luff of sail
11. Leech of sail
12. Foot of sail
13. Wishbone boom
14. Batten pocket with batten
15. Uphaul
16. Board
17. Daggerboard
18. Fin or skeg
19. Mast foot with joint
20. Window
21. Boom rope
22. Luff downhaul
23. Outhaul line

Caring for your Board

Almost all boards are made from glass reinforced plastic (fibre glass), polyester or polyurethane, and need very little looking after. Periodically your board should be cleaned with soap or a specially prepared cleaning fluid available from specialist shops to remove all sun oil, etc. Tar is an enemy of all boards and should be removed with butter, petrol or white spirit. Damage to a polyurethane board can only be repaired using a hot-air stream and polyethylene filler which is expensive, whilst grp boards can easily be mended using a glass-fibre repair kit. Polyurethane boards can be damaged by sun and heat, so they must never be left lying in hot sunlight. Surface temperatures of 50° and 60°C are reached in these conditions and your board may warp and even be damaged beyond repair.

Volume and Weight

A manageable board should weigh no more than 25 kg, bearing in mind that it has to be carried from car to water, often some distance. Before you finally decide on a board it is a good idea to pick it up and put it under your arm, simply to make sure that you can carry it!

A problem that will be dealt with later is the windsurfer's body-weight. Unfortunately, some boards do not have enough buoyancy to carry heavy surfers. Men weighing 80 kg must make sure that they choose a board with at least 200 l capacity. These boards are usually between 13 cm and 20 cm thick and at least 65–70 cm wide. A heavy surfer will only be able to get up speed if he uses a suitable board.

The Daggerboard

The daggerboard and its function are described in more detail later in the book (see p. 68). All windsurfers have a daggerboard which fits into the daggerboard case. It is longish, streamlined and flat and made from wood or plastic. The daggerboard prevents sideways drift and makes the board much more stable.

The Profile

Windsurfing is growing up as a sport and more attention is being paid to such details as the streamlining of the daggerboard. A good daggerboard, whether made from wood or plastic, is not simply a straight plank but must have a profile which is symmetrical and which tapers off at the rear. A rule of thumb is that the profile at its thickest point must be ten per cent of the width of the daggerboard. It is also important that the daggerboard is rigid so that it bends as little as possible underwater, and it must be tough to withstand knocks when the board runs aground.

The Collapse-on-Impact Daggerboard

This type of daggerboard has a decided advantage over rigid ones, not only because it prevents damage to the board on impact but also because it gives a better general performance. At high speeds a rigid daggerboard develops an unfavourable lift sideways to the water surface. The collapsible daggerboard, on the other hand, automatically retracts and causes no sideways lift at high speeds, the board remaining stable. See also the chapter on daggerboards (p. 68).

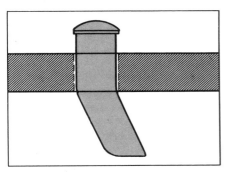

The rigid daggerboard

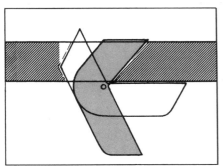

The collapsible daggerboard automatically folds up on impact and at high speeds

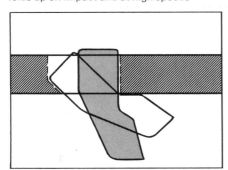

The tilting daggerboard

The Rig

The Mast

The mast is made from hardwearing flexible polyester or aluminium. Its elasticity is vital for an optimum sail profile. The flexibility of the mast is accurately calculated to give the best sailing properties in any wind. The mast should therefore be treated carefully and knocks which might damage the outer layer must be avoided. It is advisable to cover its lower end with sticky tape to protect it from knocks during transport.

The Mast Foot Joint

Newman Darby, who was the first to attach a mast to a board, solved the problem simply by using a thick rope. Hoyle Schweitzer, instead of a rope, used a universal joint, and Helbig, a German boat manufacturer, finally came up with a simple, flexible rubber joint between mast and board. This solution seems to be the best.

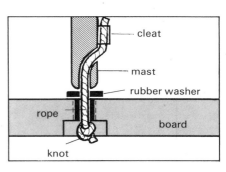

The simple rope joint used by Newman Darby

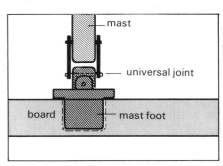

The wooden mast foot with its universal joint is easily broken

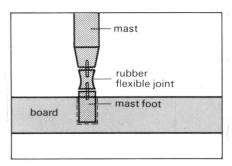

The Helbig rubber joint, the best solution

There are a great number of different joints available to attach mast to board. The hardest-wearing are made from metal, plastic or solid rubber

A cleat and a bumper are built into the front of the Mistral's wishbone boom and can be used as a handhold to move the whole rig

The Mast Foot

Problems arise as soon as an attempt is made to attach the mast foot permanently to the board; arms and legs can be bruised, crushed and even broken. It is therefore important that the mast foot is able to come free of the board if it is knocked. The best solution to this problem is seen on the Swiss Mistral-surfer with its safety line. The mast foot casing is equipped with a spring, similar to that found on ski fastenings, which releases the mast foot at a certain pressure. It is also held by a safety line so that sail and mast cannot be completely separated from the board. (See also Safety Line, p. 53.)

Wishbone Boom

The most striking feature of a windsurfer is the wishbone boom. It is constructed of two wooden booms or aluminium tubes which curve outwards and are held together by either metal clasps or rope. The wishbone boom stretches out the sail and is used to steer the board. It is the instrument of all sailing manoeuvres, and it is also your last hold on the board. A popular boom is that used on the Windsurfer. It is constructed from laminated mahogany. Its biggest disadvantage is its weight. Recently it has been proved that light aluminium booms, although they break more easily in extreme conditions, are much easier and lighter to handle. The heavy wooden wishbone boom is more difficult for beginners to handle.

It is important that the wishbone boom has a bumper at its front end to protect the board's upper surface from hard knocks. The uphaul is attached at the front and is used to pull the sail out of the water. The outhaul line at the back end is used to pull the sail flat or slacken it off.

It is a good idea to wrap some soft fabric round a bare aluminium boom to give the hands extra

holding power in strong winds.
Bicycle inner tubes can also be
placed over the boom.
The aluminium boom should be
sealed to keep the water out.
Remember this point when buying
a board.

The Sail

Windsurfers generally have a sail
with a surface area of between 5
and 6 square metres. The sail has a
mast pocket which is simply slid
over the mast, and it is stretched
by the outhaul line at the end of the
boom. It has two eyelets, one at
the bottom of the sail at the tack,
through which the luff downhaul is
fed and tied to the mast foot. This
is used to pull the luff, the front
edge, tight, while the leech and
foot lead to the clew, which has
another eyelet through which the
outhaul line is passed.
The sail may have several large
windows on its front lower surface
to give a good view to all sides.
There are pockets on the leech in
which the battens are placed. The
battens ensure that the sail
remains 'stiff' and maintains the
best profile (see diagram, p. 72).
All windsurfing sails today are
made from hardwearing, woven

The large 5.6 square metre racing sail with
mast pocket, windows and batten pockets

head
luff
leech
sail insignia
letter of
nationality
sail number
batten
pockets
window
tack
mast pocket
foot
clew

The sail is folded so that the
folds of the leech are on top
of each other and the mast
pocket forms a zigzag line

synthetic material. After use they
should be dried and then folded up
properly; the sail is folded from the
foot so that the folds of the leech
are on top of each other and the
luff forms a zigzag line. Finally, it is
folded across two or three times so
that it fits into the sail bag. A sail
which is treated properly will give
you good service for a very long
time. It will not crease and will not
produce large vertical folds. The
material dries in a few minutes, but
take time to let the mast pocket

dry completely. Loosen the outhaul
line and let the sail flap freely. If
you take good care of your sail you
will save yourself extensive
repairs. You should also examine
regularly the seams of the batten
pockets and the eyelets in the sail
and repair any damage straight
away before it worsens.

A rolling hitch, loosely tied

Rigging

Because of its simple construction a windsurfer can be rigged and ready for off in a very short time. This is the great advantage of windsurfing – its simplicity. First of all the boom rope is fastened by means of a rolling hitch or Todd hitch to a spot marked on the mast – usually with a coloured line. Then the mast is fed into the pocket so that the end of the boom rope comes out of the hole in the pocket. The sail is laid flat on the ground and the battens are placed in the batten pockets. The front edge of the sail, the luff, is pulled taut by the luff downhaul. The luff downhaul itself is fastened to the mast foot with a bowline, pulled through the eye and the loop of the knot, similar to a block and tackle, and tied with two or three half-hitches. Then the wishbone boom is fastened to the mast. To do this the boom rope is fed through the

A rolling hitch pulled tight; it cannot slip down the mast

The wishbone boom is fastened to the mast with the boom rope. The end is tied using two half-hitches

The uphaul is knotted at its upper end so that it cannot slip out of the front of the boom

corresponding eye on the boom and fastened on to the cleat on the wishbone boom. Since the mast must always lie as close as possible to the front of the boom, it is a good idea to wrap the boom rope, after it has been fed through the cleat on the boom, once more round the mast to ensure that it is firmly joined to the boom. Finally, the sail is stretched by feeding the outhaul line through the eyelet on the tack of the sail. For your first few expeditions on the water the sail should be neither too loosely

nor too tightly stretched. You will have to find out for yourself the best tension for your sail by stretching the sail so that it produces a good profile without creases on the mast and leech. Before entering the water, fasten the uphaul to the mast foot with a rubber shock cord so that it is always within reach.

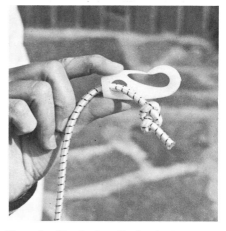

The outhaul line is placed in the cleat. Another figure-of-eight knot is tied in the end

The rubber shock cord is tied to the mast rope at the second knot from the bottom

The rubber shock cord should not be much longer than the mast rope so that it does not get in your way while surfing

A figure-of-eight knot is tied at the end of the rubber shock cord to fasten on the plastic cleat

17

The figure-of-eight knot is tied at the ends of the outhaul line, the boom rope and the rubber shock cord

Ropes and Knots

All ropes on a windsurfer are twisted, 6 mm thick and usually made from polyester. The uphaul is an exception. It is 8–12 mm thick, and very soft to protect the skin. When replacing ropes it is important to remember to singe the ends of the ropes after cutting them to prevent fraying.

Knots

The knots pictured here are the most important ones for the windsurfer. It is advisable to practise these knots thoroughly so that you can tie them easily. While the reef knot is still sometimes used (for towing), it is better to use the rolling hitch and by means of a bowline produce a simple block and tackle in the luff downhaul.

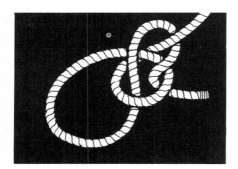

The bowline is tied in the luff downhaul and on windsurfers also in the outhaul line, and wherever a loop is needed which will not pull out and which is easy to untie

The reef knot is used to tie two ends together

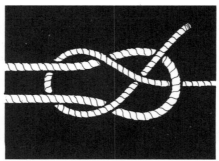

The sheetbend is used to tie together two ends of different thicknesses (e.g. when towing)

The rolling hitch is sometimes used to tie the boom rope to the mast but alternatively the Todd hitch shown above can be used. It grips as well if not better and is quicker and easier to undo

Transport

Carrying the board to the water is no problem. Any good board may be carried under the arm if you place one hand in the daggerboard case. If you find this difficult you can also place the daggerboard in the slot and hold it with both hands. The sail is more difficult. If it has to be carried over long distances, never leave the sail spread, but if the boom is attached to the mast, fold it to the mast, roll up the sail a little and tuck it under your arm. A spread sail is always carried with the mast to the wind, i.e. the length of the mast pointing into the wind; the sail is gripped over the head with one hand on the boom and the other on the mast. The rig and board are then joined together in the water. Perhaps later you might like to try a beach start, where a rig and board are fastened together on land (see p. 80).

You can never be too careful when fastening a board to a roof-rack. It is absolute madness to tie a board to a thin, wobbly roof-rack with string. A board on the roof of a car travelling at 60 mph could in certain circumstances be torn away from its roof-rack. It is, therefore, essential to use specially designed roof-racks when transporting your board. For fastening the board to the rack there are nylon straps available with special locks so that the equipment can be easily and simply lashed to the rack. You can make it even simpler by buying complete surfboard racks which can be locked. For long, fast journeys, tie the mast on top of the board and secure the ends of the mast with ropes down to the front and rear bumpers. For extra security put rope round the board through the centre board hole and then through the car with the doors open. Should the rack fail you will then not lose the board.

There are on the market special stable roof-racks for windsurfers

The sail is carried above the head so that the front of the boom is pointing into the wind

Clothing

Just as a skier wears the proper clothing for his sport, windsurfers of the future will also have their own 'uniform'. However, for now we have to be content with piecing together our outfits by borrowing from other sports, though the growing popularity of the sport has led to quite a few manufacturers producing good and useful windsurfing clothing.

The Wet-Suit

Not all windsurfers are blessed with the high summer temperatures which are found in California, Hawaii and Australia. We must also remember that even in summer perspiration formed on the body can cause chilling, especially in the kidneys when it evaporates. It is therefore advisable, even in summer in cooler climates, to wear a thin wet-suit, or at least something which will protect the kidneys. The most suitable clothing is the neoprene wet-suit. Neoprene is a foam rubber type material which has many air bubbles and is used for diving and surfing wet-suits. The material is usually lined on both sides with nylon to protect

This is completely the wrong clothing for windsurfing. You would chill very quickly in these wet clothes

the inner layer. A normal diving wet-suit, however, is not suitable for windsurfing, which is a sport where freedom of movement is essential. As in skiing, the legs and arms are mostly held bent, and you will also have to kneel, sit and lie on your board. The most important areas therefore are the shoulders, elbows, knees and feet as well as the armpits, biceps and calves. Diving suits are usually too close-fitting and made from material which is too stiff. They will restrict the blood supply to arms and legs and this will cause the surfer to tire quickly. Therefore, when buying a surfing wet-suit pay particular attention to the fit. If the suit has an outer layer of nylon make sure it has a layer of non-slip rubber at least at the knees. Also, it must have zip fasteners at the arms and legs so that it can be adjusted. For example, on a cool day you can start off with the zips closed. If after a few minutes it becomes warmer and your arms begin to swell, you can open the arm zips. This means that the circulation to the arms and the arm movements are not restricted. The cut of the sleeve is also important. If the material at the inside of the elbows and under the arms cuts in, it will restrict the flow of blood and lead to aching arms and tiredness.

It is a good idea to buy a two-piece suit so that in warm weather you can wear the 'long johns' with a windcheater, while on cooler days you can also wear the neoprene jacket to keep warm. Windsurfers who want to carry on with their sport during the winter months can wear a warm anorak over their wet-suit.

Special neoprene underclothing is also available and is very useful. The material is about 2 mm thick with the neoprene cells left open on the inside. It is very warm and allows complete freedom of movement. This thin neoprene suit, specially developed for surfing, is extremely popular because it can be worn by itself in the summer and under a normal wet-suit in the winter.

Footwear

The neoprene socks worn by divers are also useful for windsurfing. After your initial try-outs it will mainly be your feet which are constantly in the water and they must therefore be kept warm. It is advisable to wear approved neoprene socks, which usually have a zip fastener. However, these socks have the disadvantage of being quite slippery on a board. You should therefore wear over the socks a pair of gym shoes which have soft, and if possible natural rubber soles. The special windsurfing shoes which are now available are, of course, the best. They have non-slip soles and allow the foot above the heel the necessary freedom of movement.

Surfing Gloves

Windsurfers are recognisable not only by their well-balanced gait but also by their handshake, which tends to be a strong and hearty grip given with a hard-skinned right hand. After an intensive windsurfing holiday with good strong winds the skin on the hand is often as hard as that on the soles of the feet. As soon as this natural protective layer has formed gloves are not required, but for beginners simple rubber gloves such as those bought for use in the kitchen are all that is necessary.

The problem with wearing gloves is that anything between hand and boom is going to have a detrimental effect on your grip and

A windsurfing wet-suit must be made from flexible material. It is important that the sleeves and legs allow complete freedom of movement

Special windsurfing shoes allow the feet the necessary freedom of movement and prevent slipping, particularly on polyurethane surfaces

Neoprene underclothing is ideal for use on its own in the summer

Neoprene underclothing also gives an additional layer of warmth under the wet-suit on cold days

the 'feeling' for windsurfing which you get through your hands. It is best, therefore, to discard gloves as soon as possible, but to keep a careful watch on your hands when the wind is strong and rub plenty of cream into them afterwards.

Headgear

Normally no headgear is necessary, though those who wish to protect their hair may wear a simple bathing cap. Surfing enthusiasts recommend wearing a neoprene diving hat in winter, leaving just the face free. However, this has the disadvantage of impairing the hearing, which can affect balance.

If it is extremely hot, however, it is a different matter entirely. You should never forget the effect of the sun reflecting on the water, and it is therefore sensible to wear a sun-hat in summer, with a wide peak if possible. Recently experts have been recommending spray goggles, especially for tandem windsurfing, which will be discussed later in the book.

Windsurfing Theory

Handling a windsurfer is so basically different from handling a yacht that even experienced yachtsmen need some time to become accustomed to the movement of a windsurfer and its steering. Theory and practice form the basis of the sport, and both have to be learnt, so before we take to the water we must concern ourselves with a little dry-land theory.

The Wind

The sail is our board's motor, and its fuel is the wind. In order to be able to move forwards on a board, you must understand the wind, its effect on the sail and the effect of the sail on the steering.
The most important question you must ask yourself during your first practice sessions is: Where is the wind coming from? Everything depends on this. If you cannot make proper use of the action of the wind in the sail it will drive your board unmercifully before it, out into the open sea, onto rocks or towards bathing zones or other dangerous areas.

If you cannot feel the wind on your body look at flags or boats lying at anchor. If you are still unsure, take a handful of grass and throw it up in the air, or lick your finger, hold it up and feel where the wind is coming from. The direction of the wind is the most important point to be considered when you are on the water. Since the sail is your means of steering, you must be quite clear about the effect of the wind on the sail.

The Physical Explanation

On a course before the wind, that is with the wind coming from behind, the forwards movement is easy to understand since the wind drives the sail and the board before it like a leaf. However, what happens if you are not travelling before the wind, but at right-angles to it? The wind is now striking your sail diagonally from the front and is divided into two air currents. One current has to travel behind the mast to leeward round the entire sail and therefore has to go a long way. It accelerates and causes a partial vacuum, a low-pressure area, on the lee-side of the sail. The other air current, to windward, hits the sail and causes a high-pressure area. The sail therefore moves in a pressure differential between the windward and lee sides and constantly tries to yield from the high pressure towards the partial vacuum, i.e. from the windward to the lee side. We will discuss the forces at work here later in the book (see diagram on p. 72).
We now know how our wind-motor works. In order that it can give its best performance there must always be enough wind-power of the right kind. The wind which hits your sail while you are moving is not the same wind you feel on shore. It is necessary to distinguish between:

- true wind
- the wind of your own speed and
- apparent wind.

The **true wind** is the atmospheric wind which we feel on dry land, which blows a flag on a mast on the shore, for example.
The **wind of your own speed** is the wind we feel, for example, on a motor-boat travelling quickly over the sea (we feel the true wind of its own speed in calm conditions). This wind always comes towards the boat from in front of it.

The air current hitting the sail divides into two, one to the windward and one to the lee side, resulting in a pressure differential from windward to leeward pushing the sail to the lee side

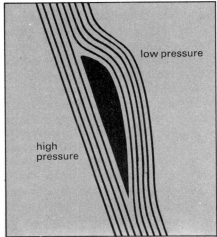

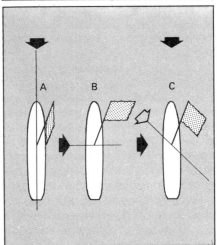

A A flag blowing in the true wind
B A flag blowing in the wind of the board's own speed
C A flag blowing in the apparent wind, made up of the true wind and the wind of the board's own speed

The **apparent wind** is a product of the true wind and the wind of your own speed. The apparent wind can only be felt when you are travelling on the water on your board, and it is this apparent wind which is vital for steering the board. It will be seen how important it is later in the book (see p. 101).

Firstly, note this rule:

To find out the true wind on the water, simply let your sail flutter in the wind – the direction of the sail tells you the direction of the true wind.

In order that the sail should work to its best effect it must always be set at the correct angle to the apparent wind, that is, the angle between the boom and the long axis of the board must be correct. The diagram on p. 27 shows the position of the sail for different travelling directions. You will notice that the boom is farther removed from the stern, the more you bear away from the wind.

Therefore, note the following:

There is only one correct sail position for each direction of travel. To find it, allow the sail to only just flap and then pull it in about a hand's width.

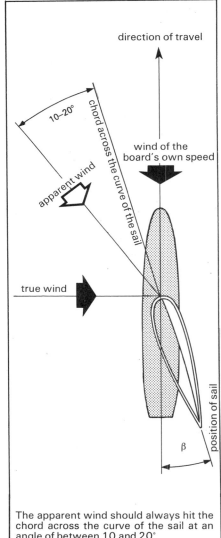

The apparent wind should always hit the chord across the curve of the sail at an angle of between 10 and 20°

Courses

Basically you can sail in any direction with your board. However, we must remember that with any sailed craft it is impossible to sail directly against the wind. We already know that the sail must always be set at a certain angle to the air current. It is not possible to sail in the sector which makes an angle of 90° at the top of the 360° circle (see diagram right – white section). Position 1 shows the position of a surfboard on the wind or close-hauled. Any attempt to get even closer to the wind would lead to the board coming to a halt. Of course, you can sail against the wind by beating up to it.

This means that you sail in a zigzag line close-hauled on tacks.

There is only one correct sail position for each course

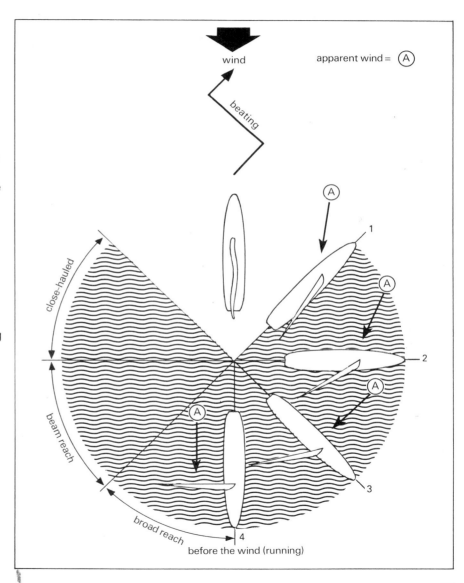

wind

apparent wind = (A)

beating

close-hauled

beam reach

broad reach

before the wind (running)

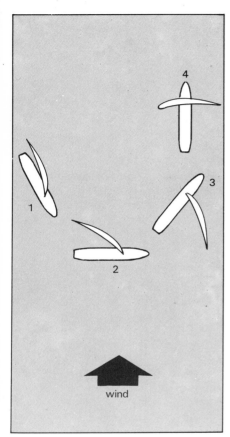

In order to sail a certain course you must always know where the wind is coming from. The course is determined by the direction of the wind

The farther you bear away from the wind, the greater the angle between the sail and the board's long axis

The individual courses are as follows:

Close-Hauled or On the Wind (1) *(Tacking)*

On this course the sail is pulled in, i.e. the angle between the boom and the board's long axis is very small.

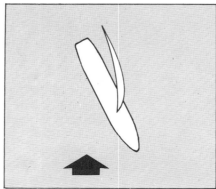

Beam Reach (2)

On a beam reach the true wind is at right-angles to the board's long axis. On this course you will almost always be travelling parallel to the waves caused by the wind and you will therefore find that you are not constantly having to battle with crests and troughs.

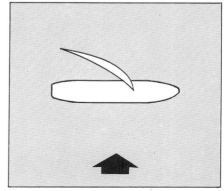

Broad Reach (3)

On this course the sail is slackened until it is almost at right-angles to the board. By slackened we mean that the sail yields to the wind pressure, i.e. the angle between the end of the boom and the stern is increased.

Before the Wind or Running (4)

As described by the term itself, on this course you are sailing away from the source of the wind. You are now sailing with the waves and it is easy to get the impression that you are travelling more slowly than you actually are. The sail is held in front of the body and you have to look through the windows to see ahead.

Beating (5)

If you want to reach a point which is directly into the wind you must sail your board in a zigzag line against the wind – this is known as beating.

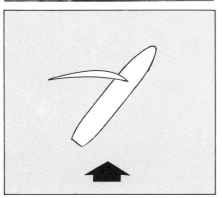

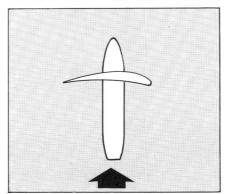

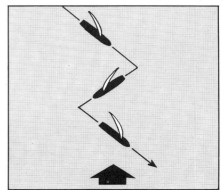

A windsurfer is steered by inclining the mast forward and aft, thus altering the sail's centre of effort and the centre of lateral resistance

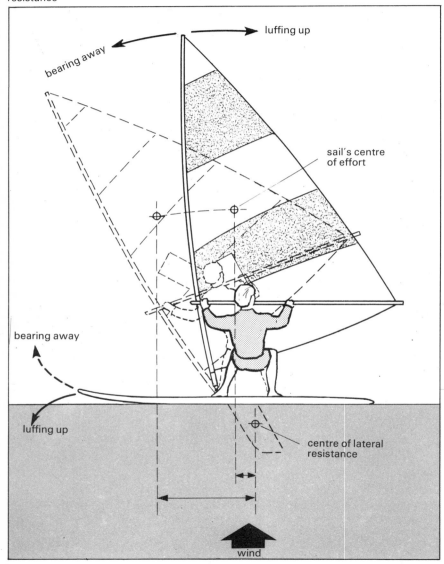

bearing away

luffing up

sail's centre of effort

bearing away

luffing up

centre of lateral resistance

wind

Steering

The basic difference between a yacht and a windsurfer is in the way they are steered. A windsurfer is steered with the sail only, without any kind of rudder. Windsurfing is therefore sailing in its purest form. With the wind in your hands you determine not only your direction of travel but also your speed, and this is why experts regard windsurfing as one of the most important developments in the sport of sailing.

The principle behind steering is extremely simple. We know that when travelling our sail has the tendency to swerve from the high-pressure side towards the low-pressure side and it therefore pulls the board with it. The daggerboard prevents sideways drift. If we imagine all the forces acting on the sail concentrated at one point on the sail's surface, this would be the sail's *centre of effort* (see diagram left). The parts in the water, i.e. board, daggerboard and skeg, also form a *centre of lateral resistance*. When travelling forwards, the sail's centre of effort lies just forward of the centre of lateral resistance. If the sail is inclined, the centre of effort is moved forwards in relation to the centre of lateral resistance, the balance is upset and the board tries to turn away from the wind; it bears away. Conversely, the board turns into the wind, it luffs up, if the sail is inclined aft and the sail's centre of effort is shifted behind the centre of lateral resistance.

Remember the two important rules:

1. **The board is steered by tilting the sail forwards towards the bow or aft towards the stern.**

2. **There is only one correct sail position for each course.**

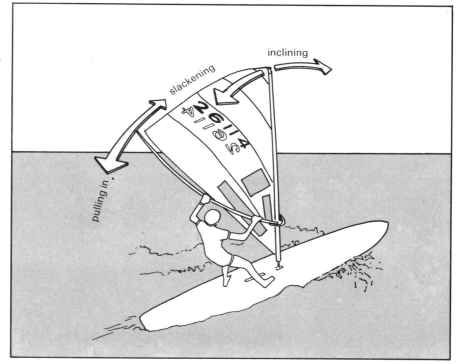

Distinguish between inclining the mast forward and aft (towards bow and stern) and pulling in or slackening the sail with the boom

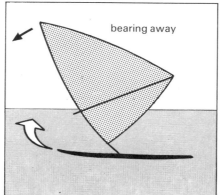

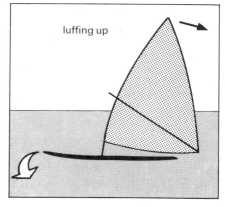

Practical Exercises

It is recommended that you take part in a windsurfing course with a qualified instructor since you will be able to practise and learn the most important movements and the function of steering on a simulator on dry land. By doing this you will not only save many tiring hours on the water, you will also be able to enjoy the company of a group of like-minded beginners and make use of safe, roped-off stretches of water and aids such as buoys. A basic windsurfing course consists of about five to seven lessons.

The Strength of the Wind

If you are not able to make use of a simulator, your first job should be to test yourself against the strength of the wind. Spread your sail as already described and place it on the ground. Stand with your back to the wind, place one foot on the mast foot and pull the sail up towards you, using the uphaul, until it flutters freely in the wind. It is a good idea to bury the mast foot in the sand – this will make the following exercises much easier. When your sail is fluttering in the wind you will be able to determine the exact direction of the wind since your sail acts just like a flag.

Remember the rule:

When raising your sail and getting underway always stand with your back to the wind.

Now try to pull the sail against the wind with both hands on the boom. In future we will call the hand nearer the mast the mast hand and the other the sail hand. If you pull a little more with the sail hand you will begin to feel the strength of the wind. If the wind is strong enough you will be able to hang completely on the boom, thereby producing a balance between your body-weight and the forces working on the sail. This playing with the wind is always controlled with the sail hand. Pulling in the sail hand, i.e. pulling in the sail, leads to more pressure on the sail and thus you have to brace yourself even more against the pressure. Yielding with the sail hand, i.e. slackening the sail, leads to a decrease in pressure on the sail and you need less strength to hold it. If there is enough wind, try to lean right back until you are hanging on the boom with outstretched arms.

Dry training is most effective. It saves hours of wet training in the early learning phase.

The simulator, the most important teaching aid in any good windsurfing school

Testing yourself against the strength of the wind – one of your first exercises on land

Balancing Exercises

Before you take to the water with board and sail you must learn all about the floating stability of your board. Do not underestimate the importance of this exercise. Before you are ready to attach the rig, you must first learn how to stand correctly on your board, how to move on it, and know where the stable and unstable spots are. After having slotted the daggerboard into the board, lie down and paddle into the water. Now try kneeling to the right and left close to the daggerboard case, holding the edge of the board with your hands. Tip the board to the right and left and test its stability. Carefully stand up with legs apart over the daggerboard case and try to turn round 360° by sliding your feet over the board. When you have managed this, try turning round 360° lifting your feet off the board, standing for a short time on one leg only. Balancing on the board is extremely important because later it is essential, for certain manoeuvres, to be able to get round the mast. To conclude the exercise, try turning by jumping round making quarter, half and full turns with each jump. Now stand on the board with legs apart and shoulders parallel to the board's

Balancing on the board without the sail cannot be practised often enough

A pupil in the process of raising his sail using the uphaul rope long axis and try to jump round 180°.

Group exercises:

Who can do a full turn the fastest?

Who can do several 180° jumps one after the other?

Who can get farthest towards the bow or stern without falling in the water?

Who can do a headstand on the board?

To complete the balancing exercises try quarter, half and whole turn jumps

To raise the sail, crouch down and grasp the mast rope with outstretched arms. Initially the sail is raised by straightening the legs only. When you are upright and the sail is almost out of the water, pull the rig towards you by bending your arms. It is important that the mast and sail are kept at right-angles to the board.

Raising the Sail

You are now ready to take your sail into the water and place the mast foot in its socket. In hip-deep water turn the board so that the sail lies to leeward (on the side of the board away from the wind), and you are standing to windward (on the side towards the wind). Now climb on to the board and take up the basic position – one foot in front of the mast at about 45° to the board's long axis while the other foot is placed on the centre of the daggerboard case. Take hold of the mast rope, crouch down and pull the sail out of the water with outstretched arms, at the same time straightening your legs. This should be done slowly so that the water has time to run off the sail. You should now be standing in the basic position on your board, back to the wind, feet in the position already described, both hands on the mast rope, the sail fluttering freely in the wind. It is important to raise the sail at right-angles to the board. Even when you are standing upright in the basic position the sail should still be fluttering at right-angles to the board's long axis. This sail position is called the *mast abeam position*.

The basic position is characterised by the sail abeam position (fluttering sail at right-angles to the board). One foot is in front of the mast, the other is on the daggerboard case. The sail is held by the uphaul close to and just underneath the boom; the arms are outstretched

Turning Exercises

We have seen that the board luffs up, it turns into the wind, when the sail is inclined aft. What you now have to do is turn the board under you by inclining the sail to one side. This is done in the basic position. Holding the uphaul with outstretched arms, lean the sail into the wind, at the same time inclining it aft. Your board should now turn into the wind and you, using small steps to correspond with the speed at which the board is turning, must now walk round the mast until your board has turned round 360° and you are back where you started. During this exercise you should not hold the wishbone boom but keep both hands on the uphaul or hold one hand out to the side to help you balance. The greater the pressure you use to push the sail against the wind, the faster your board will turn. You can make a game out of the exercise by trying to turn your board as quickly as possible. If the wind is quite strong it will travel a short distance and describe a circle of about ten to twenty metres in diameter. If the sail is handled correctly the board will turn completely automatically.

When walking round the mast, hold the uphaul with one hand and use the other to help you balance

When the board is turning; the sail is set in the direction of the wind. You make the board begin to turn by pressing the sail slightly against the wind. You then walk round the mast using small steps to correspond with the speed at which the board is turning. The hands hold the uphaul, not the boom

Getting Underway

When getting underway take up the basic position: stand with your back to the wind, one foot inclined 45° in front of the mast, the other on the daggerboard case; and let the sail flutter free. Now memorise the following sequence of movements:

1. You control bow and stern, thus determining the direction in which you wish to travel. The sail hand points towards the stern, the mast hand towards the bow (photo 1).
2. First of all take hold of the boom with the mast hand (photos 2 and 3).
3. Release the uphaul with the sail hand and let the arm hang down close to the body (photo 4).
4. While slowly turning your trunk into the direction of travel, with your mast hand bring the sail past the body to windward until the arm is slightly bent in front of the shoulder (photo 5).
5. The sail is still fluttering free in the wind and you are now looking in the direction of travel over the bow (photo 6).
6. Grip the wishbone boom with the sail hand, about 50 cm behind the mast hand (photo 7).
7. While slowly pulling in the sail with the sail hand, turn the trunk a little way back (photos 8 and 9).

Using this sequence of movements you will get underway. If the wind is so strong that you have trouble holding on to the sail, the sail hand should yield to the wind pressure. You have already practised this on land.

Remember this important rule: **Only the sail hand yields to the pressure of the wind; the mast hand does not move from its original position.**

It is essential to keep your body upright if you do not want to tire quickly during practice. Arms and legs should be slightly bent so that they can cushion any movement of the board caused by the waves. Your trunk is upright – never bending forward. Gusts of wind which push you forwards or out to the side should be counteracted by slackening the sail. Before you get underway it is most important that you are perfectly clear about the function of the mast hand and sail hand. While the sail hand is used to pull in or slacken the sail (this is the hand you sail with), the mast hand is used to incline the mast.

Basically we can distinguish between **inclining the mast forwards or aft (steering) and slackening or pulling in the sail (adjusting the sail to the wind).**

Any of the following might happen when you are getting underway:

While the sail hand is grasping the boom, the board luffs up and as soon as the sail is pulled in you fall backwards into the water.
You can avoid the board luffing up by maintaining a right-angle between board and sail until the sail hand has grasped the boom in order to pull the sail slowly in.

You cannot hold the sail – it is pulled to leeward and simply throws you off.
In this situation the sail hand must yield to the pressure of the wind, if necessary releasing the boom altogether.

The bow dips down into the waves.
If this happens you should correct your foot position: the front foot must be just in front of the mast and the rear foot on the daggerboard case.

The board does get underway but immediately luffs up, losing all the wind from the sail.
This means that during the procedure of getting underway the sail was not far enough forwards and to windward. You should counteract this luffing up by inclining the mast even more towards the bow.

As soon as your sail hand grasps the boom you lose your balance and fall in the water.
This is caused by the position of your feet (see basic position, p. 37) and your grip on the boom. Your hands should be at least 50 cm apart.

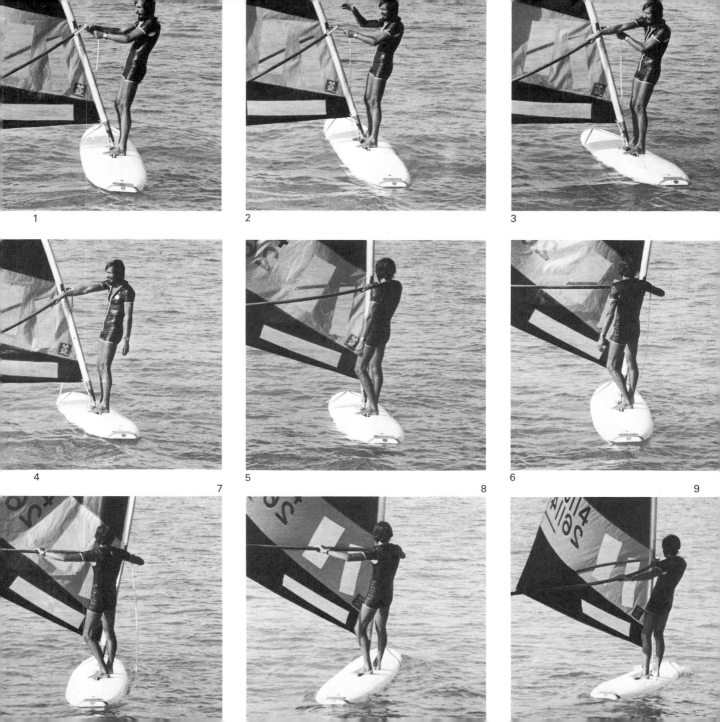

1

2

3

4

5

6

7

8

9

Travelling Position

After getting underway, take up the travelling position: knees slightly bent, arms bent and trunk leant against the wind. If the wind starts to blow more strongly you have two possible courses of action; you either utilise your body-weight and hang with outstretched arms on the boom, or you can slacken the sail with the sail hand. Practise this fine balance.

To get underway, start in the basic position and grasp the boom with your mast hand. Now release your sail hand, turn towards the direction of travel, pull the mast past your body forwards and to windward, grasp the boom with the sail hand, pull the sail in and off you go!

Steering

As soon as you are ready to get underway you must immediately start to practise steering your board since you are now in control of a sailing vessel which, like vehicles on the road, is subject to rules and regulations, quite apart from the fact that without a good knowledge of steering you constitute a danger to swimmers and other water-sport enthusiasts. You must, therefore, never practise in bathing areas, harbour entrances or busy stretches of water. You should look for a quiet spot where you are in no danger and where you cannot interfere with anyone else.
Initially you should practise sailing a wavy course, inclining the mast towards the bow and then immediately towards the stern. The board will bear away and then luff up. By doing this you will get a feeling for the movement of the sail and at the same time learn how to balance on your board with the sail in different positions.
A rule of thumb: **When you are travelling in a straight line the boom should always be parallel to the surface of the water.**
It is quite possible that when you are thrown about by the wind, waves and other water users you might suddenly completely forget which way to incline the mast in order to sail a certain course. Therefore, from the very beginning you must remember that **the direction of the wind is vital. It determines the courses open to you, so pay constant attention to the wind and remember from which direction it is blowing.**

Remember too that **bearing away, i.e. turning away from the wind, is always initiated by a corresponding bending of the rear arm, and vice versa. When luffing up the front arm is bent and the rear arm straightened.**

Going About

Up to now you have learnt how to stand on your board and how to steer by inclining the mast forward and aft. So that you can travel in any direction and get back to your starting place, it is now important to learn two basic and crucial manoeuvres, going about and gybing.

If you are sailing with the wind coming from more in front of your board than from behind your board you are on a tack (making progress against the wind). If you glance at a craft coming towards you from the opposite direction you will notice that it will have its sail on the opposite side to your sail – it is sailing on a different tack. We differentiate between starboard and starboard tack, port and port tack.

On a starboard tack your sail will be on the right side of the board, facing in the direction you are travelling. Similarly, the sail will be on the port side when it is on the left of your board facing in the direction you are travelling.

If you now change from port to starboard, taking the bow of your board through the eye of the wind, you have 'gone about'. In doing this you will find out whether or not you have taken the balancing exercises seriously since you have to go round the mast taking small steps. Your first attempts at going about will be similar to the turning exercises you have already learnt.

However, to make the whole manoeuvre run smoothly, because a smooth and easy sequence of movements will make it more fun for you, you have to learn how to make full use of the steering function of your sail.

Learn the following procedure for going about.

1. You are travelling on a beam reach, your feet in the basic position.
2. Now incline the boom towards the water, taking the mast aft.
3. As soon as the end of the boom touches the water use your sail hand to pull in the sail close to · you till the boom touches the stern.
4. The bow will now automatically turn into the wind and the board luffs up.
5. You will feel the wind leaving the sail, and at this moment your sail hand must release the boom and grasp the uphaul. At the same time you take two small steps to bring your body in front of the mast.
6. The mast hand now also takes hold of the uphaul and you stand in front of the mast, arms outstretched, your back and the bow of the board pointing into the wind.
7. Just as you have practised in the 360° turn exercises, now try, by pressing the sail against the wind, to get back into your original position. The sail will be fluttering at right-angles to the board, you correct your foot position and get underway again.

Now practise changing the wind side. Get underway, incline the boom to the water, go about while moving from one side to the other side of your board and take up your original position again ready to get underway.

If you find difficulty in getting round the mast, you should practise the 360° turn. Remember to keep your steps small during your first attempts at going about. We will deal with jumping and other ways of going about in the section on technique.

As soon as the board turns into the wind, grasp the mast rope with your sail hand

1

2

3

4

5

6

7

8

9

10

11

12

Going about – sequence of movements
(from left to right)

1. Tilt boom to water
2. Grasp uphaul with sail hand, move trunk
   in front of the mast
3. Both legs are in front of the mast, both
   hands holding the uphaul
4. Move the sail to its new position on the
   beam
5. Get underway again

The Gybe

This is the second way of getting from one tack to the opposite tack. Gybing is often considered a dangerous manoeuvre by sailors. This is because of the limitations of a normal sailing boat. It is, however, very different on a windsurfer where a gybe, well executed, is an extremely elegant and completely safe manoeuvre. For going about the board has to luff up but when gybing the board bears away (the mast is inclined forward). The sequence of movements is as follows:

1. From a beam reach you bear away by stretching the mast hand towards the bow.
2. As soon as your board turns away from the wind, release the boom with your sail hand and take hold of the uphaul.
3. While the feet are changing position from beside to behind the mast, the mast hand too takes hold of the uphaul.
4. The sail is now swinging freely in the wind, and by pulling gently on the uphaul you pull it to the other side of the bow.

9

8

7

6

5. Do not forget to change the
   position of your feet to
   correspond with the altered
   position of the sail.
Ideally, the mast should always be
in front of you and your back
should remain towards the wind at
all times. Complete the turn until
you are in your original position
and then get underway again.

1

2

3

4

5

In the gybe pictured here the mast
hand takes hold of the uphaul first. This
technique is especially recommended if
there is not much wind

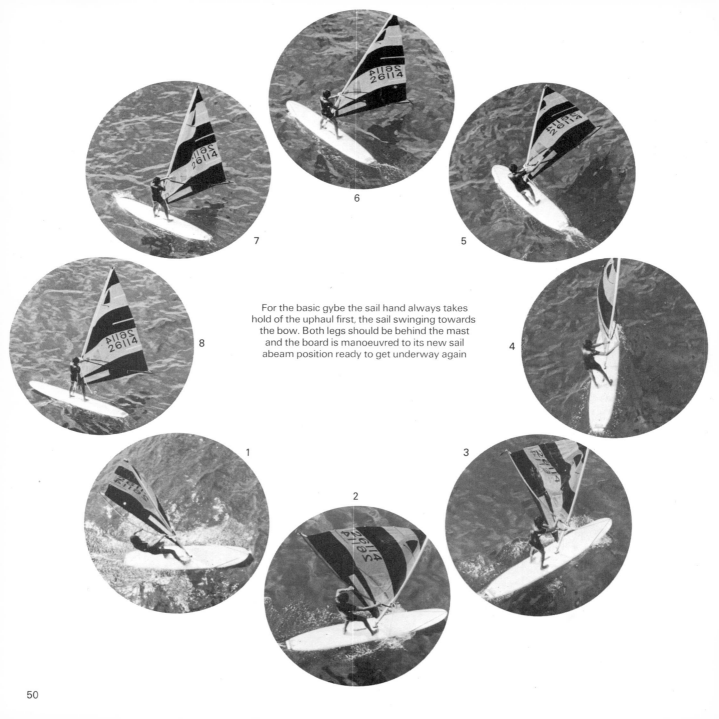

For the basic gybe the sail hand always takes hold of the uphaul first, the sail swinging towards the bow. Both legs should be behind the mast and the board is manoeuvred to its new sail abeam position ready to get underway again

50

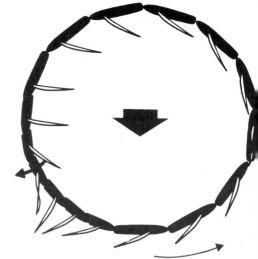

Turning a Complete Circle

You can now put your new skills to the test by joining together the manoeuvres you have learnt, in order to sail in a full circle. Take up your basic position and make sure that there is nothing on the water within a radius of 50–100 m which will interfere with your exercise. Get underway and immediately luff up. Then go about, walk round the mast to your original position and get underway again. Now bear away, gybe, complete the turn until you are back where you started and then get underway again. If you follow this sequence of movements exactly your board will describe a circle which includes all the basic sailing manoeuvres. You luff up, go about, get underway, bear away, gybe and get underway again. You cannot practise this exercise too often, going both ways, of course.

Basically you are now ready to pit your skills against wind and waves, to glide gently over calm water or to test yourself against rough seas and spray. There is no doubt that you will quickly catch the windsurfing bug, which will relentlessly drive you to the water no matter what the weather may do!

Windsurfing is basically a completely safe sport. However, traffic on water, like traffic on the roads, is subject to laws which you must not only learn but obey. For your own sake and the safety of others you must read carefully the next chapter, on Rules and Regulations.

Turning a complete circle consists of the following sequence: getting underway, luffing up, going about, bearing away, gybing, luffing up and getting underway again

Rules and Regulations

Our waterways and seas will remain areas of pleasure and safety only if those who use them are considerate and have regard for others. Windsurfers especially, who populate the water in large numbers, must be fully aware of their rights and duties.

■ On the water each windsurfer must behave in a manner which will not endanger or harm anyone else, or, as far as circumstances allow, not interfere with or annoy other people.

■ As a general rule windsurfing should not be carried out in bathing areas. Even outside these areas windsurfers must constantly be on the lookout for swimmers.

■ Shipping lanes should be avoided, as should places where craft are anchored or tied up, and harbours and harbour entrances.

■ If there is an off-shore wind you should only windsurf if you are really expert at the sport, to avoid rescue operations having to be mounted for you.

Safety Line

For your first attempts at windsurfing, especially if there is an offshore wind, your board should be equipped with a safety line. Most boards have a mast foot which detaches from the board for safety reasons to prevent arms and legs being bruised. However, if the wind is strong this can mean that rig and board can drift away from each other after a knock and before you know it you are swimming towards your sail while your board is drifting merrily away! To avoid this, a safety line is fastened between rig and board. In any case always swim to your board first, the sail will drift less swiftly and can be recovered later.

Who has right of way?

Right of Way

Windsurfers must observe the right of way rules applicable to all sailing vessels. These are as follows:

1. Each manoeuvre must be executed in good time, it must be clearly visible and it must be executed decisively.
2. Remember that the right of way may not be enforced. If a vessel which should give way does not observe the rule, you must give way yourself in good time.
3. A yacht, a sailing boat or a windsurfer on a port tack has right of way over a yacht, sailing boat or windsurfer on a starboard tack.
4. If two vessels are sailing on the same tack the vessel to windward must keep out of the way of the other.
5. Overtaking vessels must keep out of the way of the overtaken vessel.

Port – Starboard

The fundamental rule on the water is: port before starboard. To make this distinction easier it is a good idea to mark your boom with different colours. Facing the direction of travel, put a red mark on the left arm of the boom and a green mark on the right. You now need only to glance at the boom to see if you have right of way or not: red – no right of way; green – right of way.

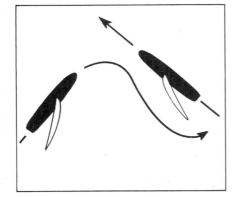

1. Port before starboard. The board with its sail on the right, facing the direction of travel, must give way

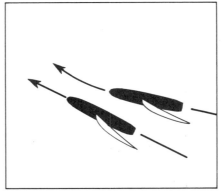

2. Lee before windward. The board to windward must give way

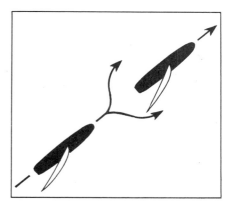

3. The board coming astern of the other must swerve either to windward or to leeward

The Weather

After your first wobbly attempts on your board you should not try to do too much too soon, especially as far as the weather is concerned. It is very important to learn how to cope with storms and also with calms. It is, therefore, a good idea to train yourself right from the start to keep a constant watch on the weather. We all know that dark clouds gathering means that the weather is going to worsen, and this is your first alarm signal. Above all, make a note of onshore and offshore winds. While you can be a little more daring with an onshore wind because you are sure of always being blown back to the shore, you should never underestimate an offshore wind. It is difficult to estimate the exact strength of an offshore wind and from the shore it is easy to make the mistake of thinking you can easily cope with it since it has very little effect on the waves close to the shore. An onshore wind, on the other hand, will ruffle the waves a lot more. Farther out, where an

offshore wind bounces off the waves with full force, its true strength can be felt, but for beginners this is usually too late.

Your board is the ideal rescue apparatus, so **in an emergency never leave your board.**

A board cannot sink. You can therefore sit or lie on it in safety and in an emergency you can even be towed.

Distress Signal

If you find yourself in difficulties, you should sit on your board as upright as possible and try to draw attention to yourself by waving both arms up and down above your head. This is the international signal for a windsurfer in trouble.

The international signal for a windsurfer in difficulties is a clear up-and-down movement of both arms above the head

Reaching the Shore Safely

In a strong wind which you cannot cope with, and also in a calm when you are unable to manoeuvre your board, the following is the procedure for getting safely to the shore:

■ Remove the mast from the slot, open the outhaul line, the luff downhaul and the outhaul, pull the mast out of the sail, fold the sail and lay the boom on the board. Now use the mast to paddle to the shore, either sitting or kneeling.

This method has proved itself over the years, and even in very strong winds and high waves you will always reach the shore safely. It is also possible to tow a colleague in difficulties to the shore.

1. The windsurfer to be towed loosens his outhaul line and rolls up his sail from the foot to the mast, tying it on with the outhaul line. The boom is collapsed against the mast.
2. The rig is now laid lengthways along the board and the windsurfer lies on top of it.

Do not make the mistake of having your colleague hang on to the back of your board. In this position if you have to beat against the wind you will find it almost impossible to move forwards, and drift out to the

With the rig rolled up you can paddle to the shore (for short distances)

You can cover greater distances if you use your mast as a paddle

side. It is much better if the windsurfer to be towed lies on your windward side and holds on to your daggerboard rope. If for any reason he cannot do this, you should loosen his luff downhaul and tie your daggerboard line to his, your board to leeward. Now you must try to beat against the wind, keeping each line of the zigzag as long as possible – after each going-about manoeuvre you must get back into your position to leeward. Another way of towing, for the more experienced, is to hold the sail by the uphaul and let the boom end slide along in the water. You will not be able to beat up against the wind like this, but you will be able to sail comparatively long stretches on a beam reach with relative ease.

In an emergency, you must above all remain calm and never lose your head. However, you can help yourself to avoid getting into difficulties by taking careful note of the special characteristics of the area in which you are sailing. This is especially important on the sea. Talk to the harbour-master and make enquiries at information offices and among colleagues and the members of the local sailing club about the points you must watch out for – especially the tides, currents, and any special features of the wind. Never underestimate the weather conditions, or a

A windsurfer being towed must always be to windward of the towing board

windsurfing expedition could well end up with you paddling to the shore. In this connection, clothing should be mentioned again. With the proper clothing you will be able to remain in the water for several hours in normal temperatures without tiring due to chilling, so always wear a neoprene wet-suit. Windsurfing is now spreading to many countries.Its novel sailing system can alarm the public authorities particularly when the sail is flat or falls in the water. Tell the water authority or coastguard what you are doing, where and when, and this will save him trouble and may ensure that you

get assistance when you really need it.

Storm Warning

There is a storm warning system on lakes and on the sea which must be heeded by all water-sport enthusiasts. Normally an approaching storm will be signalled by a flashing light. A sequence of long flashes signals a pre-storm warning and a sequence of short flashes means a storm is imminent, in which case you should make immediately for the nearest shore.

Remember – disregarding these warnings can be an offence.

The Official Teaching Programme of the German Windsurfing Schools

We now show the official teaching programme of the German Windsurfing Schools; it is hoped that this example of the degree of knowledge and skill required by the official organisations will be useful to readers outside Germany.

The Basic Diploma

At the end of the basic course in windsurfing in those schools affiliated to the German Windsurfing Association, students enter for the Basic Diploma in Windsurfing.

The course consists of instruction in the following points:

1. Short introduction to the sport of windsurfing
2. Description of the board and its individual components
3. Correct foot position (simulator)
4. Raising the sail (simulator)
5. Position for getting underway (simulator)
6. Understanding the wind (simulator)
7. Procedure for getting underway (simulator)
8. Travelling position (simulator)
9. Steering (simulator)
10. Going about (simulator)
11. Gybing (simulator)
12. Rigging
13. Rolling up the sail in an emergency
14. Carrying board and sail
15. Balancing exercises on the board in the water
16. Turning exercises round a buoy
17. Getting underway on the water
18. Bearing away and luffing up
19. Going about
20. Gybing
21. Before-the-wind course (running)
22. Turning a complete circle
23. Ideal sail position
24. The different courses
25. Windsurfing in a group
26. Trimming the sail
27. Knots
28. Transporting the board (roof-rack)
29. Methods of steering
30. Right-of-way rules
31. Local rules
32. Weather
33. Clothing
34. Your own safety and the safety of others
35. Distress signal
36. Rescue operations
37. First aid

The examination for the Basic Diploma has two sections, theoretical and practical.

Theory

The candidate has to answer fifteen questions taken from the list shown on pp. 60 and 61 (the answers are given here too). In this part of the exam his knowledge of points of safety, right-of-way rules, the distress signal and rescue procedures, as well as all points concerning windsurfing itself, will be tested.

Practical Section

1. Rigging the windsurfer correctly.

2. Getting underway and sailing a straight course on a beam reach.

3. Stopping on a beam reach (simulated emergency).

4. Going about and gybing using the correct sequence of movements.

5. Bearing away from a beam reach until he is on a true before-the-wind course (running).

Questions for the Basic Diploma in Windsurfing

1. What should a windsurfer wear?	Extensive protective clothing, e.g. neoprene wet suit.
2. What is the international distress signal for surfers on the water?	Moving both arms up and down above the head.
3. What safety precautions should be taken in a strong offshore wind with regard to the board's equipment?	A safety line should be fastened between rig and board.
4. What are the three most important rules dealing with right of way for sailing vessels and thus for windsurfers?	Port before starboard; lee before windward; the vessel coming up astern must give way
5. Where should you not windsurf?	In bathing areas, at harbour entrances, in harbours, where crafts are at anchor or tie up, in shipping lanes
6. Which water-sport enthusiasts should a windsurfer be especially watchful for?	Swimmers
7. When practising on the water what should you especially bear in mind?	The falling range of your mast.
8. How are storm warnings given? And what should you do?	By a flashing light. Long sequence of flashes, pre-warning; short sequence of flashes, imminent warning. You should make your way immediately to the shore.
9. Which knot is used to tie the boom rope to the mast?	Rolling hitch, or Todd hitch.
10. When transporting a board on a roof-rack what must you remember?	The roof-rack must be stable and capable of carrying at least 40 kg.
11. How do you see in front of you when you are sailing on a before-the-wind course (running)	Through the windows.
12. How do you start the procedure for going about on a windsurfer?	By tilting the boom towards the water and at the same time pulling the sail in with the sail hand.
13. Define the concepts lee and windward.	Windward is the side towards the wind, lee is the side away from the wind.
14. How do you trim your sail for strong and gentle winds?	The sail is tensioned using the outhaul line and the luff downhaul. For a gentle wind the sail is given a belly, for a strong wind the sail is flat.
15. How do you stop your board quickly?	By letting the rig fall into the water, or doing a stop gybe.
16. Which knot do you tie on the outhaul line after it has been fed through the cleat?	Figure-of-eight knot.
17. How do you reach the shore in a strong offshore wind if you cannot hold your sail?	Bring the rig down and paddle with the mast.
18. Where is the sail laid before it is raised on the simulator?	To leeward.
19. Why is the uphaul tied to the mast at its bottom end with a rubber shock cord?	So that it always remains within reach.
20. What is the purpose of the skeg?	It keeps the windsurfer on a steady course.
21. Why should the mast foot detach from the board if it is knocked?	To prevent arms and legs being crushed.
22. What is the rope called which is used to tie the boom to the mast?	The boom rope.

23. Why must a windsurfer wear protective clothing?	Because he is in constant contact with the water and therefore must take precautions against hypothermia.
24. Why should beginners not practise in an offshore wind?	Because they will usually underestimate the strength of the wind and can quickly be driven out to sea.
25. What must you take special note of on waters that are not familiar to you?	The special characteristics of that particular area, e.g. currents, shipping lanes, etc.
26. Why is practice on a simulator so useful?	Because you can practise and learn all the movements in safety
27. Why are buoys used in windsurfing schools?	To keep the pupils in a safe area.
28. How can you tell a fishing or a naval vessel?	They have green or red flags.
29. In an emergency why must you always remain on your board?	Because the board is an ideal rescue device; it is unsinkable.
30. What does 'luff up' mean?	'Turning into the wind'.
31. How do you initiate a gybe?	By bearing away (inclining the mast forward).
32. Which wind do you sail by?	The apparent wind.
33. When getting underway, which hand is used to grip the boom first of all?	The mast hand
34. What does 'bear away' mean?	'Turn out of the wind'.
35. How do you get on a running course (before the wind)?	By bearing away.
36. Two windsurfers are sailing with the wind on the same side. Who has right of way?	The one to leeward.
37. A vessel is approaching another from behind. Which should give way?	The vessel coming from behind.
38. Two boats are sailing towards each other on different tacks; which one must give way?	The boat on the starboard tack.
39. What is the purpose of the daggerboard?	It prevents sideways drift.
40. Which knot is used to tie a loop, e.g. for towing?	Bowline.
41. In a calm how do you get to the shore with your board?	By paddling with the mast.
42. If you want to be towed what must you do?	Take rig down, lie flat on your board and hold on to the daggerboard line to windward of the board towing you.
43. Which vessels have absolute right of way on the water?	Naval vessels and fishing vessels.
44. When must you *never* go on the water with your board?	At night.
45. What must you remember to do when windsurfing in shallow water?	Raise the daggerboard

Crouch down and jump up, stretching the body

Conditioning

Windsurfing makes use of the whole body. Arms, legs, shoulders and stomach muscles are particularly put under stress. It is essential to be generally fit, and you can achieve this by spending a little time and effort on exercising.

Conditioning for windsurfing can be divided into two sections:
1. Warming-up and loosening-up exercises.
2. Exercises designed to strengthen the muscles and increase stamina.

Special demands are made on you when you are standing, sitting, kneeling or lying on your board in positions you are not used to. The following exercises are designed to increase the body's ability to cope with these special stresses and strains. The training must include not only exercises for strengthening the muscles, but also exercises designed to help you cope with the static stresses and strains on muscles and groups of muscles (fingers, forearms, thighs and calves).

When you are windsurfing, it is the fingers and forearms especially which can soon tire. During a long period at full stretch, for example in a race, the body can quickly become fatigued so that movements which are second nature to you normally become cumbersome and tiring.

Just as an engine needs to 'warm up' before it can give its best performance, your body and muscles must also be warmed and loosened up before you can expect them to perform properly.

Warming-up and Loosening-up Exercises

Let us say that you have unpacked your board from the roof-rack, carried it several hundred metres to the water and you can already feel your forearms beginning to ache. If you then immediately take your board on to the water you will certainly be back on shore after five or ten minutes, massaging your swollen forearms.

Therefore, before getting into the water you should take time to do a few warming-up exercises:

1. Jump on the spot – crouch down and jump up with body outstretched.
2. Do a little shadow-boxing while making a fist with the

Shadow boxing

hands and then shaking them loose.

3. Make fast arm circling movements, alternately forwards and backwards (to increase circulation in the hands).

4. After these exercises slap the underarm muscles with the backs of the hands to massage them.

5. Hang on a branch, post, door-frame or any other suitable ledge and 'feel' the stretching you will experience on your board. Do not, however, overdo this exercise – it is only meant to help you warm up.

Exercises for Two People

1. The partners stand opposite each other, hands on a broomstick (wishbone boom), feet together. Now pull on the stick and crouch down. Then both stand up together.

2. One person grasps the broomstick between the hands of the other person. Now try to pull the broomstick away from your partner.

Once you are well loosened up (with a good flow of blood through the body), you can put on your wet-suit. It is quite in order to perspire a little since it is better to set off on the water a little too warm than try to haul up the uphaul with cold shaking hands and get underway while shivering and trying to keep warm. Of course, you should not go to the other extreme and set off thoroughly exhausted and perspiring profusely!

Training for Racing and Long Tours

A short warming-up session of three to five minutes is all that is required before a normal windsurfing expedition. However, if you are racing and expecting to take part in several heats and therefore are going to be on the water for a few hours, I would recommend that you increase your warming-up session to ten or twenty minutes, carrying out the following exercises:
1. Warm up as above.
2. Crouch down and stretch out your legs alternately (like a Cossack dancer).
3. Crouch down and move forwards by taking long jumps.
4. With legs slightly apart, circle your arms backwards and forwards while bending the trunk forwards.

Fast arm circling, backwards and forwards

Slowly crouch down and straighten up

63

'Cossack dancing'

Crouching jumps forwards

Arm-circling and trunk-bending

5. Sit on the ground, pull up your legs and stand up without using your arms, then sprint forward.
6. Do several press-ups; in between you could hang on a post, or similar.

The exercises should be carried out at least half an hour before you go into the water. They should be repeated until you are feeling just a little tired. Then rest for ten minutes, completely relaxed, breathing deeply. You can then put on your wet-suit and you are ready for the water.

Regular Conditioning and Strength Training

In cool climates windsurfing is a seasonal sport. The ideal winter equivalents are skiing and long distance running. General fitness will be increased considerably by cycling and cross-country running. Apart from this there is a special type of training for windsurfers, using simple apparatus which you can make yourself. This consists of a short, round piece of wood about 30 cm long and about as thick as a wishbone boom. You also need a

Press-ups

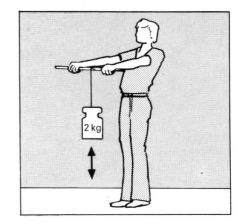

piece of cord about 1.5 m long, and a small sandbag which can be filled with 1–2 kg of sand. The sandbag (filled with not more than 1 kg of sand to begin with) is fastened with the cord to the middle of the piece of wood, and the exercise consists of lifting it by the cord with outstretched arms. To begin with you can let the cord run over a door handle so that you are pulling horizontally, just as you would on your board. Later, the sandbag is lifted with outstretched arms directly from the floor.

This exercise has a dual purpose: it strengthens the arms, and especially the shoulder muscles, and it also improves your grip. As is described in the chapter on the different grips (see p. 95), the boom should not be gripped with a constant firm hold but you should continually change your grip. The longer your hand is firmly closed round the boom in one position, the longer the circulation is cut off from your forearm, and this can lead to cramp.

There is a special piece of equipment available from specialist shops for strengthening hand and forearm muscles. It is made from two plastic handles joined by a steel spring, but the same effect can be achieved using a tennis ball. The ball or the spring

grip is pressed for about six seconds and released, and you then stretch your hand. This is repeated for about ten minutes. It is incredible the difference you will feel if you do this for ten minutes twice daily for two months.

It is important that you are thoroughly warmed up and suitably and warmly dressed if you go windsurfing on cooler days or in the spring when the water is still very cold. Initially you will find that you have to carry out the special exercises to prevent cramp and tiredness in legs and arms, but later, as an advanced windsurfer, you will find that the exercises to warm up the body are enough. The sport of windsurfing itself will help to keep you fit and this makes windsurfing an ideal training medium for other sports.

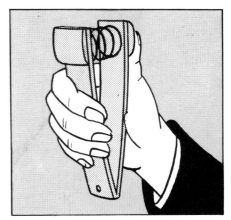

Top: You can strengthen your arm muscles enormously by using this simple apparatus

Middle: At the start pull the weight over a door handle so that you are pulling horizontally

Bottom: You can strengthen your finger muscles by using this spring grip available from specialist shops

Windsurfing Technique

The Board

Illustrated here are two different types of board.

The **Windglider** is broad in front and narrow aft.

Advantages:
The Board's profile is technically suitable for all courses. The board is distinguished by its broad bow. This prevents it cutting under the waves and this is especially advantageous when running before the wind.

Disadvantages:
Boards with narrow sterns sink deep into the water when planing. Also, they are not stable and are inclined to go off-course on courses across the waves. The narrow stern also has a detrimental affect on the general stability of the board, especially for beginners.

The **Mistral-Surfer** is relatively narrow in front and has a broad stern.

Advantages:
The board is very stable on the water and, especially for heavier windsurfers, presents an ideal ratio of buoyancy to volume because of its wide planing area.

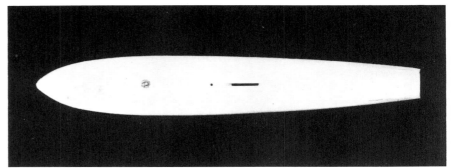

The Windglider, broad in front and narrow aft

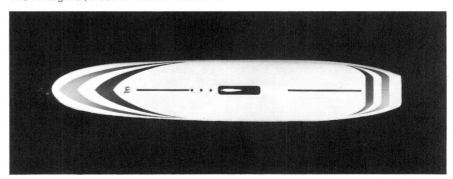

The Mistral-Surfer, with its broad stern

Disadvantages:

The board's profile requires a good deal of skill from the surfer, especially when running before the wind, since the decreased buoyancy area at the bow can lead to it cutting under the water.

Most boards, however, are somewhere between these two extremes. Also there are many high-speed boards on the market which are very long and narrow. These 'windsurfing balance beams' reach speeds which are only marginally faster than normal boards, mostly on broad reach courses. They are extremely difficult to manoeuvre and are therefore intended for 'hot-dogging' rather than general sailing.

The Daggerboard

As already mentioned earlier in the book, special attention must be paid to the shape of the daggerboard. A correctly profiled daggerboard is vital not only for the speed of your board but also for its general performance. For example, an incorrectly positioned daggerboard will cause capsizing. This is why on a Windsurfer it is raised at least halfway on reach courses. Raising the daggerboard on all other boards is also advantageous on a broad reach or when running. The board will be easier to steer.

The Daggerboard Profile

It is relatively easy to make a well-profiled daggerboard yourself from marine plywood. The drawing on the left shows the ideal profile with a thickness/width ratio of ten per cent.
From the sketch make a pattern which includes half of the daggerboard shape. Now lay this on your daggerboard and sand it down until it is the right shape. Lacquer the daggerboard several times, sanding down between each coat until the surface is clean

The pattern for the daggerboard profile can be enlarged to the size of the daggerboard

Schwert-Profil-Schablone ©1977 by Ernstfried Prade

and smooth. Finally, sand the surface once again with a very fine grit sandpaper.

The Storm Daggerboard

Windsurfers who happen to live in windy areas or who prefer to windsurf in strong winds are recommended to use a storm daggerboard. The reduced surface area makes it travel through the water more easily. Storm daggerboards do not cause a detrimental lateral pressure and can be constructed to fold up if they hit the bottom. Normally the surface of a storm daggerboard is arranged more astern than a normal daggerboard so that the centre of the underwater surface of the board lies more astern. This is because a board at high speed will lift its bow out of the water, resulting in a new centre of lateral resistance. The diagram on p. 69 shows a universal storm daggerboard which you can make yourself from marine plywood. The daggerboard is pushed up into the case from below and tied to the mast foot with a rubber band. It is rounded off on its upper edge to ensure that it will come out of the case if it receives a knock.

The Tilting Daggerboard

The tilting daggerboard developed by Tilo Riedel is the ideal compromise between a normal racing daggerboard and a storm daggerboard, the only disadvantage of this construction being that it pokes out of the board in both the upright and tilted positions.

Windsurfing without a Daggerboard

If you want to feel for yourself the effect of the daggerboard, leave it on shore for a while. You will feel the instability of the board as soon as you climb onto it. Even getting underway presents difficulties. However, you will be even more surprised by its gliding ability on a broad reach. The board will lie still and keep exactly on course, leaving you to concentrate fully on wind and waves. To beat back to his original position an expert would heel over his board a little to windward, thereby achieving sufficient lateral surface from the edge of the board to enable him to beat up against the wind.

The Skeg and its Function

We already know that the skeg is

When windsurfing without the daggerboard, carry it on your arm

responsible for keeping the board on course. It can, however, be an extremely interesting exercise to try windsurfing with a shortened skeg or even no skeg at all (hot-dogging). Since board manufacturers have not yet taken this point into consideration (with the exception of the Mistral-Surfer with its collapsible skeg), it is worth experimenting for yourself. For high-speed surfing a very long, narrow skeg is recommended. You will be able to twist and turn your board to your heart's content if you remove the skeg or place it lengthways along the board, as is the case on the Windglider. The Windsurfer skeg is a compromise between these two types.

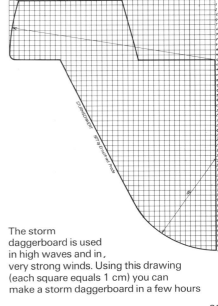

The storm daggerboard is used in high waves and in very strong winds. Using this drawing (each square equals 1 cm) you can make a storm daggerboard in a few hours

The Sail

The Sailcloth

Almost all the materials used for windsurfing sails are extremely strong. Depending on the individual manufacturer a cloth between 135 and 155 grams per square metre is generally used and for storm windsurfing the cloth may be up to 180 grams per square metre. It is worth treating your sail very carefully. For example, you should never fold and pack away a wet sail. Let it dry off on the mast, pull the battens out of the pockets and finally roll it to the mast. You can take your sail to a sail-maker to be repaired, or you can buy special yarn from him and do small repairs yourself. The vulnerable spots on a sail are the batten pockets and the eyelets on the tack and luff.

The Cut of the Sail

The sail is trimmed with the outhaul line which is used to trim it flat or full. In general a windsurfing sail is cut so that when it is stretched with the outhaul line there is a pull on the leech and foot which bends the mast. The bending of the mast has the effect of pulling flat the belly cut into the

sail. If you are going to windsurf often in a strong wind you should have the following adjustments made to your sail.

■ At the head of the sail the mast pocket should be reinforced so that the tensioning of the leech is distributed over a larger area and not concentrated at one point only, the tip of the mast.

■ A foot downhaul should be positioned beside the luff downhaul to give support to it and at the same time enable the sail to be tensioned over a wider area behind the mast.

■ When windsurfing in strong winds you should also make sure that the windows are large enough. A suggestion would be to move the windows farther back and to position the lowest window as close as possible to the foot.

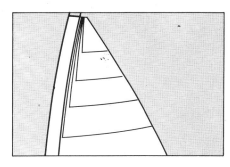

The sail head is strengthened round the mast pocket

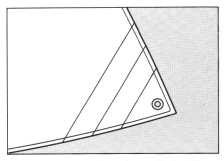

The tack is strengthened to make it stiff

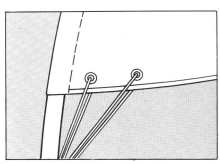

A foot downhaul is positioned near to the luff downhaul to stretch the sail downwards

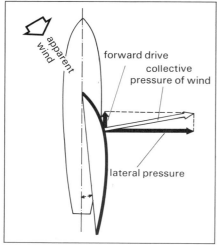

The forces working on the sail

A sail trimmed flat

A sail trimmed full

Trimming the Sail

We already know the rule: sail trimmed full for low winds, sail trimmed flat for strong winds. The reason why we use a flatter sail in strong winds is because a full sail develops an enormous pull and it will take every ounce of your strength to hold it. Tests have shown that a full sail can be used in strong winds provided that the fullness is in exactly the right place. If a very strong wind blows up and bends the mast and if the sail is cut badly, the belly will be pushed right out towards the leech, resulting in an unfavourable relationship between the forward drive and the lateral pressure. In the diagram above left we can see the profile which will result in a maximum forward drive with a minimum lateral pressure. You should also be careful not to pull the sail too tight. You will put too much strain on the seams and eyelets and you will lose your sail profile. Always keep at least 3–5 cm in reserve between the tack and the end of the boom.

Most sails with a maximum foot of 2.5 m have a 15 cm area of adjustment. In other words, when flat the sail is pulled up to 5 cm from the boom, while for low winds it is pulled up to 20 cm from the boom. While on normal sailing vessels the trim of the sail can only be altered by means of several different mechanisms, on a windsurfer you are able to alter it by using your own body. For example, the leech can be made tighter or slacker by pulling down with the sail hand. Also, by inclining the sail to windward you reduce the sail surface area and can thus handle stronger winds.

Kite Sailing

While a sailing boat with its permanent mast must always tilt to leeward, a windsurfer is in the position of being able to pull his sail to windward in order to make it function like an aerofoil. As soon as you pull the mast over you and hang on the boom against the wind, the sail produces not only forward thrust but also lift. This lift is especially helpful to heavier surfers. Used correctly in a strong wind it can reduce the body-weight and, ideally, eliminate it altogether.

The technique of kite sailing is actually quite simple. Ideally, you should be sailing close-hauled; then crouch down and slacken the sail a little with the sail hand, at the same time pulling the mast over you, i.e. you tilt the mast to windward. The stronger the wind, the more weight you will be able to put on the boom. Light surfers can even lie flat above the water with body outstretched. As in all the other windsurfing positions, the function of the sail hand is vital to maintain a balance between the force of the wind and your body. If the wind suddenly drops after a gust you can either pull in the sail or bring yourself quickly back over the board, using the knee push. To do this you push your knees under

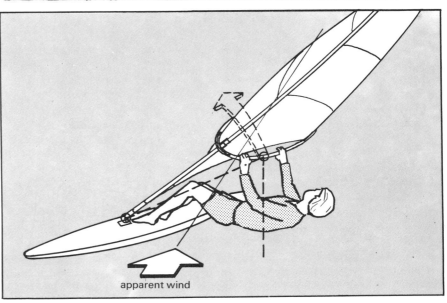

apparent wind

Heavier surfers use the knee push technique to get their body-weight quickly back on the board's long axis and avoid falling off the side of the board into the water

the foot to bring your body's centre of gravity over the board.

Storm Sails

It is pointless to use a normal sail of 5.6 square metres if the wind is stronger than Force 5–6. Storm sails have been specially developed for this purpose. They are between 3 and 4.5 square metres and are therefore smaller and much easier to handle. It is best if the sail's centre of effort cannot sink too low and the leech

is automatically tensioned. A storm sail has no battens and is easy to handle even in the strongest winds. This type of sail works better in stronger winds, generally Force 5 and upwards, than the 5.6 square metres sail since its leech does not flap about causing unfavourable lateral pressure. Thus you can travel faster with less effort. Of course, this is only true for close-hauled courses.

Light Weather Sails

Many sail manufacturers also produce light-weather sails with a surface area of about 7 square metres. In order to be able to use one of these you will have to insert an extension to your mast between its lower end and the mast foot. Light-weather sails are recommended to all who live in areas where the wind is generally very light. However, if you try to use one of these sails in a Force 4–5 wind you not only risk your mast breaking, you will be able to do very little actual sailing.

The three sizes of sail: right, the racing sail, 5.6 square metres; centre, a 4.5 square metres all-round sail; left, a small storm sail with a 2.8 square metres surface area, also used for teaching beginners

Getting Underway in Strong Winds

One of the most difficult parts of windsurfing in strong winds is actually getting underway. The board has to be set in motion from a stationary position in extreme weather conditions. To do this you will need excellent balance and, above all, you will have to carry out the special sequence of movements faultlessly. Remember how you tested your strength against the wind on dry land and how the sail hand played a vital role by regulating the amount of wind in the sail, thus controlling the balance between your own body-weight and the wind pressure on the sail. When getting underway in strong winds it is a question of 'taking' only as much wind as can be counterbalanced by your body-weight. This quantity of wind, which is different for everyone and depends on your own body-weight and strength, is hauled in with the sail hand. In other words, from a fluttering position in the wind the sail is pulled in closer to you. We already know from the normal procedure for getting underway that the position of the board in relation to the sail is crucial for success. Similarly, when getting underway in a strong wind an exact angle

between sail and board must be maintained.

This is the best way to do it:

1. Take up your basic position.
2. Pull the uphaul and bear away a little, i.e. you force your board with its fluttering sail on a broad reach course, the sail now fluttering near to the bow.
3. You now grasp the boom with your mast hand as usual and pull it past your body backwards to windward so that the end of the boom is pointing upwards.
4. While inclining the mast you must be very careful that the board does not luff up but maintains the correct broad reach angle to the sail.
5. Grasp the boom carefully with your sail hand, trunk turning towards the direction of travel.
6. Crouch down. While the sail hand pulls the sail in, the board luffs up on a beam reach.
7. You should now start to move, and the faster you go the more the pressure of the wind in the sail decreases. You can now pull the sail closer in to you with your sail hand.
8. As soon as you have your board well under control on a beam reach, you can try to bear away. If the bow starts to luff up and the board tips over to the side you must counteract this by moving your weight forward and leaning farther out.

If after getting underway you intend taking a broad reach course, you should raise your daggerboard before you set off. This not only simplifies the procedure for getting underway but, as we know, it helps to stop the bow lifting up. If you also bend your knees during the phase when your sail hand is pulling in the sail, this will make your getting underway procedure easier, mainly because when you bend down and lie back the wind is more easily directed from the sail over your legs and the foot of the mast to the board, which will then shoot forward.

Up to now we have been talking about a manoeuvre which is carried out as quickly as possible using every ounce of your strength. Now try exactly the opposite.

When you are getting underway in strong winds the mast is not on the beam; the sail is much nearer to the bow

Remain as long as possible with sail fluttering to windward, keeping your board under control. Slowly pull in the sail with the sail hand, a hand's width at a time, and thus begin to move forward. You will notice that you will be able to do this with very little effort.

Note: **Getting underway in a strong wind should be carried out step by step, slowly and in a controlled fashion.**

The most important prerequisite is that the board must be on a beam reach to broad reach course, the mast inclined 45° to windward.

Foot Positions

If you look at the table of foot positions on p. 92, you will notice that in strong winds the feet are farther apart. Almost always on close-hauled, beam reach and broad reach courses the front foot is positioned beside or even in front of the mast. When you are getting underway in strong winds your front foot should be at an angle of 45° beside the mast or, better still, about 10 cm in front of the mast. As soon as the wind pressure begins to build up in the sail, you can conduct it over your front foot and on to the board, pressing the bow, which tends to luff up, out of the wind on a stable course.

Pulling Yourself Up Out of the Water

Pulling yourself up out of the water has always been part of windsurfing technique. Those who have not tried it are still a long way from getting the most from their sport. In hard-fought races this enjoyable manoeuvre becomes a necessity when you want to lose as little precious time as possible after a fall to windward.

You are travelling on a broad reach or beam reach. Your body is just about touching the water. To pull yourself up successfully the wind will have to be Force 4–5, depending on your weight. Gently slacken your sail, then let your body gradually drop into the water, thereby braking your board. Continue to do this until only your head and arms are above the surface of the water. Your feet must remain on the edge of the board. During this manoeuvre the wind pressure decreases noticeably because of the tilt to windward. Make sure that your sail does not touch the water since this will make it very difficult for you to haul it up again. Now bend your outstretched legs until their backs are almost touching the edge of the board; in other words, do a knees-bend under the water. Pull in the boom as far as possible with

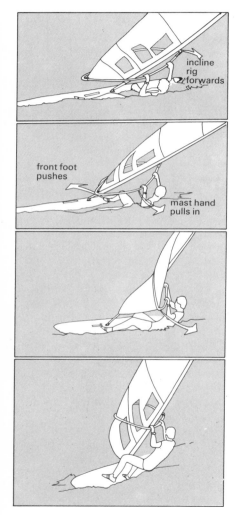

incline rig forwards

front foot pushes

mast hand pulls in

Pulling yourself out of the water will only be successful if the front foot pushes the board away from the wind while the sail hand pulls in

your sail hand and your body will be slowly lifted up. Try first of all to get your knees on to the board and then pull the rest of your body after them. You may kneel on the board for a short time. Once your centre of gravity is over the edge of the board you will have no trouble in standing up.

The Procedure for Experts

The whole procedure becomes much more difficult if you do not bend you knees but simply fall back into the water. The legs remain apart and almost straight on the edge of the board. You must be in complete control of your sail and continually adjust it with your sail hand so that it remains filled. At the next gust of wind hold firmly on to the boom (this will take a little strength) and let yourself be pulled up by the wind pressure. The front foot must press on to the board to keep it on course. This manoeuvre is, of course, more suitable for light windsurfers.

Possible Problems

During this procedure it is especially important to make sure that your board does not luff up. As

soon as the wind hits the sail from the front it will push it towards the water and it will be impossible to raise yourself.

If, when practising this manoeuvre, you glide into the water at too high a speed, it can happen that your feet are torn away from the edge of the board. Since you now have no hold on the board the sail usually falls into the water and you have to climb on to the board. If this happens, however, try holding the sail up while swimming and attempt to get your feet back on to the edge of the board and then, with a lot of effort and patience, you may well succeed in pulling yourself up. If you stand too far out on the edge of the board for too long it may capsize to leeward, so try to get back into the centre of your board as quickly as possible. Pulling yourself out of the water is in no way an acrobatic stunt like those seen in freestyle acrobatic windsurfing, but should be part of the normal repertoire of any windsurfer who wants to make full use of all the opportunities offered by the sport. In races it can save a competitor precious seconds and, apart from this, if a competitor falls to windward it can become a spectacular new start for him, rather than an ugly exit from the race.

During the beach start procedure the front foot is braced against the mast foot

The Beach Start

If you think you always have to carry your board into knee-deep water, you should try getting underway direct from the shore on a long sandy beach – the beach start. This can be done anywhere where there is a sandy stretch of beach. You hang the daggerboard over your arm or leave it on the beach, unscrew the fin or push it up. You now position yourself as if you were getting underway in a strong wind, the board on a broad reach course. The beach start can only be carried out if the wind is in a certain direction, namely parallel to the coast to slightly offshore. The sand should be dry under your board. Rock your board gently to and fro so that it is not braked by hollows in the sand, and proceed as follows:

1. Place the board on a broad reach course.
2. Raise the sail and use your mast hand to pull it to windward.
3. Now get into position on the board, bracing your front foot on the joint.
4. While pulling in the sail with your sail hand, lift the board off the sand by crouching down and straightening up again.

5. The movement of your body now makes the board begin to glide slowly along the sand.
6. As soon as you begin to move you will increase speed rapidly. You must now concentrate fully on the moment when you hit the water.
7. As soon as the bow touches the water the board is slowed down by the wet sand and the water itself.
8. You must now immediately place all your weight on the stern so that you are not flung forward with the rig. The transition from beach to water is the most crucial stage in the operation. You will probably fall flat on your face a few times till you have learned how to cushion the violent jerk and steer the board from the sand into the water in a smooth glide.

If there is enough sand you will be able to whizz along the beach as far as thirty or so metres. Since this is only possible by bracing the front foot on the joint you should always wear gym shoes. However, only those boards with a detachable mast foot are suitable for this procedure.

The Turn Tack

There are a great many turning manoeuvres which can be used by experts, and these almost always involve the sail being pulled over to windward. While in the procedure for going about which you learned as a beginner the boom is inclined towards the water and the sail immediately pulled in to the stern, for turn tack the sail is forcibly swung over the stern to windward after the boom has touched the water. Your board will then luff up, the speed at which it does this depending on the type of skeg you are using since the skeg brakes the board's turning movement. The turn tack is used to make the board turn faster. Swinging the sail over the stern has another advantage in that after changing the side of the wind the sail is automatically in the correct position, i.e. it is at the correct angle to the board.

The Jump Tack

The tricky point for most windsurfers when going about is getting round the mast. The new technique of the jump tack came about quite simply because of the need to be able to turn as quickly as possible when travelling across the waves so as to get the waves on a new tack before being buried by them. This fast sequence of movements carried out between the waves was developed and refined until it became the jump tack as we know it today.

For the turn tack the sail is pulled over the stern to windward

1   2   3   4   5   6

The Jump

The problem is that any uncontrolled jump on the board invariably leads to a ducking. Although you may be able to take off well, the landing on the new windward side is a different matter and takes a great deal of practice. This, then, is the sequence of movements for the jump tack.

1. As usual the mast is first of all inclined towards the stern until the boom end touches the water. Both legs are behind the mast, and sail hand and mast hand are the normal 50–60 cm apart.
2. The sail hand now slowly pulls the sail in so that the boom comes to lie directly over the stern. The arm nearest to the stern is now stretched out and you must push your body towards the bow because you are now close to the direction of the true wind and standing to the side of and close to the mast would lead to you falling over to windward.
3. The mast hand takes hold of the uphaul while the sail hand pulls the sail over to about 50 cm from the board's long axis.
4. You now jump up with both feet turning at the same time. The rear foot lands in front of the mast and the front foot lands in the rear foot's original position.

The jump tack is one complete movement. If you jump too soon the movement will be awkward since you will have to press the sail against the wind in order to be able to get underway. This can be avoided if your sail hand pulls in the sail, thus accelerating the board's turn through the line of the wind. The board will turn farther during your jump and your mast hand can initiate the getting underway procedure immediately after landing. If your rear foot lands too far forward, which is often the case with beginners, you must push it against the daggerboard case before starting to get underway.

7   8   9

1

2

Preliminary Exercises for the Jump Tack

For the jump tack the sail is pulled over to windward and the windsurfer rounds the mast with one jump. A carefully controlled take-off is vital to ensure a safe landing

You are sailing close-hauled, arms outstretched, trunk upright. Your front foot is beside the mast. Now try to jump about 10 cm high with both legs, being careful not to land too far over to the side ! Before jumping, crouch down a little and cushion your landing by bending your knees. Now go about, pull over the sail and jump again. After you have practised this several times and feel confident, try landing on the new windward side. During the jump use the free sail hand to help you balance. The more powerful your jump off and turn, the faster and therefore safer will be your landing on the other side.

3

4

5

1   2   3   4   5   6

The Step Tack

This turn is mainly used in light winds up to Force 3. It is characterised by its exceptionally harmonious sequence of movements which leaves onlookers on the beach spellbound with admiration – the whole movement is executed in a split second with a single step (*not* a jump).

1. Begin by pulling over the sail.
2. Both feet are together on the daggerboard case.
3. As soon as you are in the wind, your mast hand, which becomes the new sail hand, goes round the sail and takes hold of the other side of the boom. The front foot takes one step to get over to the new windward side and you now have the sail between your legs. As soon as this foot has taken up its new position, the other foot also swings round the sail to windward.
4. While the rear foot is going round the mast your sail hand, now the new mast hand, grasps the boom and pulls it forward, both movements being carefully synchronised. You are now in your new position for getting underway.

The last phase of the step tack is getting underway. Changing from one tack to another is a smooth, continuous movement in which the board describes a small circle and immediately glides away on the new tack.

The step tack is characterised by a calm, harmonious sequence of movements. The mast is rounded with a single step

The foot which rounds the mast first must stand on exactly the same spot as that on which the other foot stood

The Overhead Tack

The most spectacular way of changing the sailing direction is the overhead tack. This turn, invented by the Stickl brothers, is different from the other going-about manoeuvres in that you do not go round the front of the mast but duck underneath the sail from the lee side to windward.

While the sail hand, now the new mast hand, takes hold of the boom on the new windward side, the windsurfer ducks underneath the sail

This is the sequence of movements for an overhead tack:
1. By inclining the boom you luff up while pulling the sail gently over the stern.
2. As soon as the wind leaves the sail and the bow is standing in the wind, bend down.
3. Push the sail towards the wind with your mast hand.
4. Crouching down, duck under the foot and
5. Try to grasp the other side of the boom immediately with your sail hand.

When practising the overhead tack you should tie the boom in its lowest position. Ducking down and through to the new windward side is extremely difficult at first. You will find that your head tends to get stuck on the foot and therefore you cannot reach the boom quickly enough, causing either a capsize to windward or the sail to fall to leeward. It is best to practise the manoeuvre first of all on land. Raise the sail and try, by inclining the mast forwards and lifting up the foot, to get from one side to the other. The farther forward you incline the mast, the easier you will find it. Well executed, the overhead tack is the fastest way of going about. To do the manoeuvre correctly you need to be exceptionally agile and have excellent balance and it is therefore often regarded as belonging to that branch of the sport known as hot-dog surfing, where tricks and stunts are the order of the day.

The overhead tack can almost be seen as an acrobatic feat. The windsurfer must slip underneath the sail to the new windward side – all in a split second

1   2   3   4   5   6

9

8

7

6

5

4

3

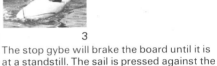

2

The stop gybe will brake the board until it is at a standstill. The sail is pressed against the wind and pulled over the bow to the other side

The Stop Gybe

The wide stern laboriously obeys the rudder, the skipper turns his yacht into the jetty. He knows that he must begin this manoeuvre in plenty of time – about twenty metres from the jetty. His calculations are a little on the tight side. Although he uses every ounce of strength to hold his yacht back, his landing can clearly be heard. This is one possible description of a yacht coming into a jetty.

Did you know that sailing boats have to turn into the wind in order to 'stop'?

A windsurfer is much more manoeuvrable, quite apart from its natural drag-anchor, the sail, which in an emergency can simply be dropped into the water. A surfer has several ways of 'stopping' his board. The most common is the stop gybe.

Stopping and Gybing

This manoeuvre can be used to stop a board on all courses except a hard broad reach or before-the-wind course. As the name implies, the board is brought to a standstill before the gybe. The gybe does not have to be executed immediately afterwards.

The sequence of movements is as follows:

1. You are sailing close-hauled, for example on a port tack, your front foot positioned beside the mast foot.
2. If you suddenly press your sail against the wind with your sail hand, your board will stop. It is important when doing this that you push first with the sail hand and then with the mast hand.

3. As soon as you slow down, pull the sail to windward with your mast hand and, with your foot near the mast, push the point of the board through and under the sail. The gybe begins.
4. The stern describes an arc through the wind, and the board goes on a starboard tack. Take hold of the boom with your new mast hand and correct your foot position. You can now get underway.

It is especially important to learn how to push against the wind with the sail to leeward. To do this, instead of pulling on the boom as normal, you press the sail against the apparent wind, i.e. the wind of your own speed and the true wind. You press just until the board is no longer travelling in a straight line; if you continue to push the sail against the wind after 'pulling up', the board will begin to turn quickly and out of control and will also cut under the water. The best way to carry out this manoeuvre is therefore to let go with your sail hand and hold the boom with your mast hand only. This method of stopping and gybing is best carried out in winds up to Force 3 and 4. If you need to stop in stronger winds, it is better to simply drop the sail into the water, though professional windsurfers who have to manoeuvre in a very tight space behind the starting line to try to get to the best starting position use the stop gybe even in strong winds.

The Stop Gybe in Strong Winds

Pressing the sail against the wind in winds greater than Force 4 is extremely difficult since gusts will most probably make you lose your balance and fall into the water. It is better, in strong winds, to take hold of the boom with your mast hand in front of the mast to leeward, then press with the sail hand against the wind and quickly pull the sail over the bow with the mast hand. Only extremely expert windsurfers will be able to master this manoeuvre. The board will cut under and this requires exceptionally expert footwork. Also, the pull working on the mast hand must be carried over both legs and on to the board for the turn to be induced. However, it is worth trying out this method of stopping on a windy day. At least you can practise turning your board in heavy waves. The ideal preparation for the stop gybe is the 360° turn exercise. To start with you simply hold the mast rope, and if you make your turns very fast you will be very close to a stop gybe.

1

2

3

4

5

6

The Swing Gybe

The gybe is one of the most beautiful manoeuvres in the sport of windsurfing. The swing gybe is a very special variation.

For this manoeuvre the sail is very quickly shifted from one tack to the other. It can be executed in very light breezes, but is mainly used in strong winds. In the main it is used to steer when running before the wind. A windsurfer who is struggling on a before-the-wind course in a Force 4 or 5 wind will find his steering very limited. Yet obstacles have to be avoided, waves have to be met at exactly the right angle and the position of your tiring feet must be changed. The swing gybe is carried out as follows:

The sail can also be swung round without taking hold of the mast rope. The mast hand is used to swing the sail round

6

5

4

1

2

3

8

7

6

5

1. You are on a true before-the-wind course, i.e. your legs are either placed on a slant as in the table on p. 92 or they are to the left and right of the daggerboard case. You are holding the sail so its centre of effort is directly above the joint so there is no chance of it falling to right or left.

2. Grasp the uphaul with your mast hand – this must be done extremely quickly or the sail will be pulled out of your hand.

3. In our example you are sailing on a port tack. With your mast hand on the uphaul you now pull the mast towards starboard. The board will then luff up to port.

4. As soon as you feel the board begin to luff up, release the sail hand, simultaneously pulling the uphaul and the sail towards you with the mast hand.

5. The sail now swings over the bow. It automatically turns round 180° and the sail hand catches the sail by the boom and pulls it to port so that the mast hand can reach the boom.

The crucial part of the swing gybe is the jerk on the mast rope which causes the sail to turn quickly.

Position of Feet and Legwork

Windsurfing makes great demands on arms and legs. While the hands must keep hold of the boom, the legs are moved about to enable you to maintain a well-balanced stance, which also saves them from tiring quickly. At the start you will probably be afraid of moving about on your board. However, you should practise the correct foot positions as early as possible to ease the constant pull on arms and trunk and to discover the best position

A swing gybe is only possible on a running course if the sail is held so that its centre of effort is above the joint, the mast being tilted. The mast hand takes hold of the mast rope and pulls the mast aft towards you. The sail now swings round and lands in front of your body so that mast and sail hands have simply to reach out and take hold of it.

4

3

2

1

for transmitting the power of the wind in the sail over the body and on to the board. The position of your feet dictates to a large extent how long you are able to stay on your board. In the table on p. 92 you will see the most common foot positions for the different courses in different winds. Heavier

Positions of the Feet on Different Courses

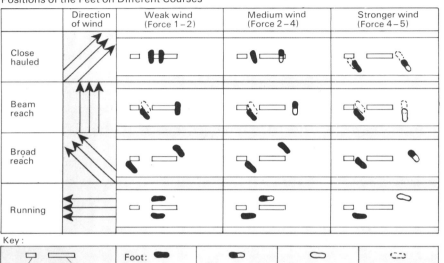

	Direction of wind	Weak wind (Force 1 – 2)	Medium wind (Force 2 – 4)	Stronger wind (Force 4 – 5)
Close hauled				
Beam reach				
Broad reach				
Running				

Key:

Mast foot Daggerboard	Foot: Full weight	Half weight	Very little weight	Windsurfers over 70kg

1. When you are windsurfing in an upright position, both legs should be slightly bent. The feet are never parallel but always at an angle to each other. The ideal position is for the front foot to be parallel to the board's long axis and the rear foot to be at right-angles to it. This well-balanced position is taken from the sport of fencing and has been tried and tested over the years.

2. If you are sailing long courses and you have to maintain a certain foot position, in order to prevent cramp you must keep bending and straightening your body.

3. In strong winds you can counteract tiredness by supporting yourself alternately on toes and heels.

4. You will be able to lean back or hang out to the side of your board only if you keep as much as possible of the soles of your feet on the board's surface.

5. If you are kneeling on a running or broad reach course, remain on your toes as far as possible.

6. Bracing your feet against the mast foot must be kept for emergencies only. Beware of letting this become a bad habit.

windsurfers, of course, will use slightly different positions to light surfers. While light surfers are able to stand right out towards the edge of their boards, heavier surfers must always beware of tipping their boards over and this makes it necessary for them to keep their weight as near to the centre of the board as possible. The position of the feet is altered for two reasons:
1. To keep balance
2. To trim the board.
Keeping balance is automatic. You change the position of your feet

instinctively if, for example, you stray too far towards the edge of the board and it threatens to overturn. You also use your feet to counter the effect of gusts of wind or strong waves. A good windsurfer will constantly change his foot position. Just as a skier compensates for the uneven snow surface by cushioning the bumps with his legs, windsurfers too use their legs in every manoeuvre to keep their boards steady and to find the stance which is the least tiring.
Note also the following:

7. You should never windsurf barefoot, but always wear gym shoes for protection and to give yourself a better stance; if possible, the shoes should have natural rubber soles.

8. Until you gain confidence always move with very small steps (sliding your feet along the board). Later you can try little jumps to find out where on the board you can safely land with your whole weight.

9. By walking round on the board you will discover where the unstable spots are. For example, on a running course it is worth trying to move your feet as close to the stern as possible. This is not only great fun but is an extremely difficult balancing exercise.

10. Heavy surfers who find it difficult to move quickly on the board are recommended to mark their safe standing positions with red sticky tape. This is placed round the mast to behind the daggerboard case and shows the area where you can safely risk moving with one or both feet.

The Trim of the Board

Changing the position of the feet becomes somewhat more difficult when the purpose is to keep the board in a good position on the water. Basically, it is a question of countering or consciously changing the centre of lateral resistance.

Trimming the board is closely connected with the correct use of the rig; for example, on a broad reach course you will only be able to get maximum effort from your rig if at the same time you keep the whole length of the board in the water by keeping your feet in the correct position. As has already been mentioned, on a broad reach and running course the bow tends to climb out of the water. This is due firstly to a lift working on the daggerboard, secondly to a lift on the board itself causing it to plane, and thirdly to the windsurfer

moving his weight aft.

If we look at the above diagram we see the angle of a board to the water on a fast broad reach course. It shows clearly that the stern, sunk deep in the water, becomes a sort of brake. You can avoid this by moving your weight forward. If the construction of your board allows, you can also move the mast foot farther forward so that the pressure on the sail works farther forward on the board and the windsurfer's weight is also moved farther forward.

On broad reach and before-running courses remember the following important rule: Length means speed.

In this connection, those boards which have a broad gliding surface and therefore better gliding

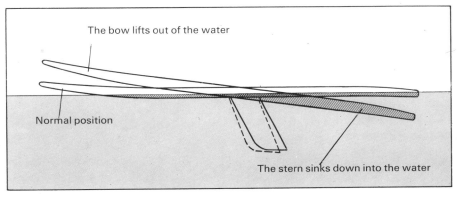

The bow of the board lifts out of the water – it planes. The stern sinks down into the water and has a braking effect

The bow lifts out of the water

Normal position

The stern sinks down into the water

qualities must be preferred.
On close-hauled courses the centre of lateral resistance can be consciously altered by heeling over.

Some boards have special edges which can be used as the lateral resistance by pressing them into the water, either to leeward or to windward. Heeling over is naturally only recommended for expert racing windsurfers. It serves no purpose in normal windsurfing. The following paragraphs deal with the different foot positions to give the best board trim on the different courses.

Close-Hauled (Tacking)

Your board will not plane on this course and the waves have to be negotiated with as little loss of speed as possible. You must therefore stand as near to the centre of the daggerboard case as possible, thus holding the board horizontal. You will also sometimes move your weight forwards so that the bow climbs the waves without cutting under them. In stronger winds the front foot should be moved farther towards the mast foot and edge of the board in order to maintain the horizontal position of the board.

Beam Reach

You will travel much faster on this course and will not have to battle constantly with the troughs and peaks of the waves, so you will not find it difficult to move your front foot farther forward to keep the entire length of your board in the water.

Broad Reach

This course requires great agility. As the waves catch up with you from behind, you have to lean back and sometimes even move your front foot farther aft so that the bow quickly moves up the wave without braking the board too much. Straight afterwards you must put all your weight on your front foot to press the board down into the next trough and then immediately move your weight aft so that the bow does not cut under the next wave. Travelling on a broad reach, therefore, means that the body-weight is constantly fluctuating between bow and stern. Of course, this only applies if the waves are large. In very strong winds this backwards and forwards movement is not necessary since the point of the bow is usually lifted so far out of

the water that there is no danger of it cutting under the waves.

Before the Wind (Running)

On a running course, especially if the wind is strong, it is a good idea to kneel down on the leg on the sail side. This has the advantage of bringing your body's centre of gravity as close to the board as possible so that you are not being pushed forward by gusts of wind from behind. This position also helps the board's trim because your body-weight is brought nearer to the bow. On a running course there is the danger of cutting under, especially if the sea is choppy. As on a broad reach, you must lean quickly aft into the trough.

Regular grip

The Grips

There is sunshine, beautiful wind, good general conditions and yet after ten minutes you cannot hold the boom any longer! This situation is only too common. Your hands let you down. This dreadful disappointment can be avoided if you learn early how to use all the different grips at your disposal. Normally you will begin with the **regular grip** and then change to the **reverse grip**. You can either change both hands simultaneously or change one hand at a time so that you are for a short time using the **mixed grip**. Racing windsurfers use the **elbow grip**, especially on close-hauled courses. When this grip is used the sail can be pulled right in and you are at the same time resting your forearm muscles. The underarm grip is also used on close-hauled courses; it entails putting the boom under the armpit and letting the arm hang loosely over it, thus resting all the arm muscles.

Apart from these grips, the position of the fingers can also vary. Normally the hand grasps the boom so that the four fingers are on top of it and the thumb underneath it. Equally well, the thumb can grip on top of the boom with the fingers; this grip is especially useful for the sail hand. When using the elbow grip you are resting your finger muscles by stretching them out and pressing the palm of your hand against the boom.

The reverse grip is used mainly for the mast hand since it can grip the boom much more satisfactorily without the awkward bending of the wrist

On both the regular and reverse grips the thumb can be rested by placing it along the boom

Reverse grip

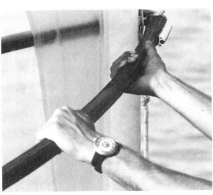

Mixed grip

Elbow grip

Surf Sailing

Waves and breakers give a new dimension to windsurfing. Windsurfing in breakers requires courage, skill and excellent board control. Only expert windsurfers are recommended to tackle metre-high waves and try to use not only the power of the wind, but also the force of the waves.

If your daggerboard is not collapsible I would recommend that you use a storm daggerboard and if there is enough wind you will also get on better with a storm sail.

When surf sailing you must remember the following points:

- Prepare yourself and your board for getting underway and then watch the rhythm of the waves. After a series of high waves there are always several lower waves which then gradually increase in size. Make use of this rhythm when getting underway. As soon as the last high wave has broken go backwards into the water, pulling your board behind you, ideally with the mast foot already in place and with the board turned over so that skeg and daggerboard are on top.

- When you are up to your hips in the water turn the board over quickly, climb on, raise the sail and immediately get underway. The wind will usually be onshore so that you are beating up through the waves.

- As soon as you see the first broken wave approaching you, place your weight on your rear foot, letting the board lift up at the bow. Brace your front foot against the jolt which will almost throw you over when you reach the foam.

- Always try to have enough wind in your sail and, above all, avoid coming to a stop. You must keep your board constantly on the move and meet each wave with the bow of your board.

- Accelerate and make straight for the waves. If the wave does not break move your weight far aft, climb the wave, slacken the sail and jump into the next trough, cushioning the jolt with your whole body and your legs.

- Now you must pull the sail in and get underway again.

- Two-metre-high waves which break just as you are climbing them are impossible to deal with. You should jump as far off the side of your board as you can to keep clear of the board which will be tumbling about in the wave.

- Having safely arrived behind the waves, first of all take a little break and observe once again the wave formations so that you get to know the high and low wave cycle.

- You now sail towards the shore on a broad reach. Slacken your sail so that the rolling waves can catch up with you. Just before the wave lifts up the stern, pull the sail in again so you can travel with the speed of the wave. To start with you should adjust your speed so that you stay between two waves. The wind pressure in the sail will decrease since the wind of your own speed becomes so strong that it cancels out the true wind. From this moment on you steer your board with your legs.

- Try to sail diagonally down the waves, never at a right-angle to them. Your feet are behind the daggerboard case so that the board does not cut under in troughs. If you want to surf right up to the shore you will obviously need a collapsible daggerboard.

- If you are on a beam reach it is a good idea to leave your daggerboard behind altogether.

Surf sailing

Broad Reach

The dream of every single windsurfer is to glide weightlessly over the water, leaning right back, the body only a few centimetres above the water. While on a close-hauled course you have to battle hard with the waves and brace yourself against the enormous sideways pull of the sail, it is on a fast broad reach course that your knees will really begin to knock!

If the wind is Force 4 or stronger you should raise your daggerboard or fold it up. Above all you must be extremely careful when handling the rig since many attempts on a broad reach course end up in a skid fall or a capsize fall.

On a broad reach course the board easily glides along with the wave

The Skid Fall

Why this fall is so common is easy to explain. To bear away the sail must be inclined forward and you pull the sail in with the sail hand. The board now turns in a large arc away from the wind and it is during this phase, when the board is turning, that most windsurfers forget to synchronise the movement of the sail with the new wind direction. They are on a broad reach course and if there is a sudden gust of wind from behind they will be blown face down. When bearing away, especially in winds stronger than Force 4, concentrate on your sail position. The apparent wind should always flow on to the chord across the curve of your sail at an angle of 10°–20°. This means you must constantly pull in the sail while bearing away.

There is also another problem you should be aware of. The farther you bear away, the more your speed will increase. Remember – the apparent wind is made up of the true wind and the wind of your own speed. Since your board is travelling considerably faster than on a close-hauled or beam reach course, the wind of your own speed has also considerably increased. This stronger wind hitting you from the front diverts the apparent wind farther forward too. You sail and steer exclusively with the apparent wind. Since this is now coming from farther in front of you, you must bear away even more to achieve the necessary angle of 10°–20° between sail and apparent wind. Therefore, to reach maximum speed you must constantly bear away.

The Capsize Fall

At high speeds the daggerboard develops a lift which lifts the board. You will begin to lose your footing, and the board heels over. It makes no difference if it heels to windward or to leeward, since at that moment the sideways pull of the daggerboard increases and the board begins to tip over. It is this turning movement of the daggerboard which causes the capsize fall and there is no cure for it. Even if you move right over to the edge of the board you will still lose control. In this situation it is better to jump immediately from the board so that you are not struck by the daggerboard or skeg when the board suddenly turns over.

Capsize falls can be avoided by raising the daggerboard. A swivelling daggerboard makes this easy to do.

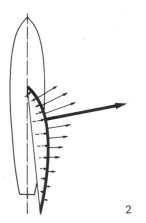

On a close-hauled course the pull is directed more abeam while on a broad reach it is directed more towards the board's long axis

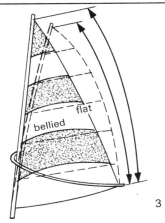

The individual pressures working on the sail. We can, however, concentrate all these pressures into one combined force

Because of the bending of the mast the upper part of the sail becomes flat – the leech curves out

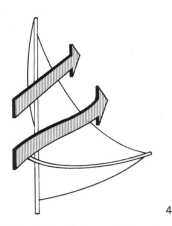

The wind whistles past the sail without imparting any noticeable forwards thrust

The Wind Pressure and Your Sail

Diagram 2 shows the forces working on the sail, the length of the arrows indicating the actual strength of the pressure on the various parts of the sail. Now imagine the total forces concentrated in a single arrow and this gives you the collective pressure of the wind and its direction. Diagram 1 shows that this collective pressure on a close-hauled course is directed more abeam of the board, while on a broad reach course it pulls more in the direction of the board's long axis. We can now see that on a close-hauled course your arms have to hold a strong sideways pull resulting in a correspondingly smaller forwards thrust, while on a broad reach course almost all of the pressure is translated into the forwards thrust.

Mast Curvature and Sailing Technique

The biggest variable on your rig is the mast. Unfortunately we cannot control this and its flexibility, which is an advantage to the beginner because it automatically helps to get rid of superfluous wind, becomes a disadvantage to the speed enthusiast or racing expert trying to keep his board going as fast as possible or trying to get closer to the wind. Diagram 3 shows a normally trimmed sail.

The measurement between the top of the mast and the tack, measured along the edge of the leech, is about 440 cm. In Force 4 winds or thereabouts the mast bends back, shortening the distance between the tip of the mast and the tack to around 400 cm, the leech still being the same length. It is clear that the curve of the leech becomes quite different since it now curves out. While with the sail shown in diagram 3 you can get very close to the wind, you are forced to bear away because of the bending of the mast, since on the upper part of the sail at least the angle of incidence of the apparent wind is nil; it is coming so far from the front that the sail collapses. This phenomenon occurs mainly on close-hauled courses. While the lower part of the sail remains all right the upper part begins to flutter, i.e. it forms a counter-belly. The only thing you can do to counteract this is to increase your pull on the end of the boom. In a race, therefore, when beating up against the wind, always pull down on the boom end with your sail hand. By doing this you will tighten the leech and thereby maintain as far as possible the ideal sail profile.

Windsurfing Racing

Equipment

The biggest advantage racing windsurfers have over their yachting colleagues is their simple craft. Those who have had to get a large yacht ready for a race will value the simple structure of a windsurfer. Yet you will be making a big mistake if you do not take time to prepare your equipment properly before a race. Always go through your checklist thoroughly.

The Ropes

Is the running hitch correctly tied, is the boom rope chafed anywhere ? Is the luff downhaul tied so that it can be adjusted for any wind direction ? The same applies to the outhaul line.

The Boom

Are the cleats still fast ? Will the boom take sufficient weight in strong winds ? Does the outhaul line move smoothly on the boom end so that the sail can be adjusted while travelling ?

Other Important Parts

Is the mast still fully flexible, with no cracks in the mast foot or the boom rope area ? Is the daggerboard still firm and strong on its thinly profiled sides ? Are both the skeg screws firmly fastened ? Are the seams of the batten pockets in order ? Are the eyelets on the tack and clew in good order ? It is especially important to check these things before races where you are given a board, since you will not be using your own trustworthy craft.

Fitness

Windsurfing is one of the few sports where enormous numbers of calories are used up in a very short time, so accustom yourself to the wind and the particular sailing area slowly, and take your training in stages. Every windsurfer knows the feeling when his tongue gets furry and his mouth becomes dry after the first few gusts of wind and initial going-about manoeuvres. Prepare for this lack of fluids by drinking more than usual before each race.

Before going into the water remember this important rule :

Never try to battle against wind and waves without sufficient training.

Why Arm Exercises ?

Those who take to the water overheated, having pulled their board from the roof-rack and gone into the water two minutes later, know the answer. They will find that their hands let them down after about ten minutes on the water. The cause is lack of blood in the forearms. When racing you must do everything possible to prevent this critical state, taking time to exercise on land. The best exercises for this are press-ups and then pull-ups on a bar. It is important that you have a good flow of blood through your arm muscles before tackling the wind.

Precautionary Measures

Half an hour before the start, take your board on the water and let off steam for ten minutes – especially if the wind is strong. Then relax : stay on the water and lie flat on your board, loosening your arm muscles by making fists with your hands and then shaking your arms.

Tactics – Your Best Weapon

Again and again clever tactics are confused with unfair tactics. A brilliant tactician is often branded with unfair behaviour simply because the accuser does not understand the rules. Anyone who does not take full advantage of the rules when constructing his tactical plan is actually the guilty one. Begin by observing the wind. When are you going to change tacks when beating up? When you think you have sailed long enough with the main bunch or when you feel the wind change direction? Success depends on these and other considerations. We cannot go into details regarding the racing rules here since space does not allow, but it is obvious that each participant must know and understand each and every rule. It goes without saying that you must know the rules before you can abide by them and actually make use of them for your own advantage. Many windsurfers forget that the rules are also there to be used. What do inside position, a safe position to leeward, to have the wind taken out of your sail mean? The rules must be the basis of any tactical plan and without this knowledge you are not going to win. Take note particularly of the special rules which are given out before the start of the race. Take note of all flag signals and if something is not clear, then ask about it. That is what the race organisers are there for. Never start off with any doubts in your mind.

The Changing Wind

In our sport everything depends on the airstream whose direction can be easily determined by experts when others have difficulty in feeling it at all. As it becomes stronger everyone can feel it. Then you must beware: strong winds are changeable and these changes in direction will help ensure a hundred metre lead for the tactically clever windsurfer. One person may feel the wind change direction in his beard, another sees it on the water and a third may feel it on his whole body. You can learn how to read the wind, and it is not so difficult. Also you have on your board the best wind direction indicator there is – your sail swinging free. Position yourself with your legs apart on either side of the mast, sail abeam in the basic position, and place one hand on the mast about 20 cm above the boom. Your arm is outstretched, the sail is fluttering free in the wind and the board is at right-angles to it. Stand like this for at least five minutes, concentrating on maintaining the right-angle between sail and board by using your legs. Cushion the impact of the waves with your whole body. The more stable your position, the more you can concentrate on your sail and the hand holding it.

Now, by removing any pressure on your legs, notice whether or not the board turns, keeping your hand firmly on the mast. You will see that the mast has a tendency to turn to one side. Transmit this turning movement to the board. Get a fix on two points on the land over the bow and stern. You can now discover the angle of the wind turning. You must, however, carry out this procedure over several minutes. This control of the wind is absolutely essential before any race and is better if carried out just before the start because it will determine if you are going to get underway on a port or starboard tack, whether you are going to take up your starting position in the front row or second row and whether you will beat up against the wind in long or short stages.

The tactical considerations are so many and varied that they are not discussed in a separate chapter but are included in the following sections on the different stages of the race itself.

The Start

Before entering the water, trim your sail according to the wind you are anticipating in the next heat. In the intervals between heats correct the trim of the sail, carry out a trial run and make any final adjustments. A rule of thumb: keep the sail too flat rather than too full. A flatter sail is easier to handle, allows you to get closer to the wind and requires less effort to

hold it. In order to do all this you must get into the water in good time.

The Starting Line

You must first of all come to terms with the starting line, which should lie at right-angles to the direction of the wind. In the diagrams below we can see that you will have a decided advantage if you see that the starting line is slanted and choose the correct starting position. Take your board between mark 3 and the starting boat, take two points over bow and stern and observe the sail fluttering free; if it

is not at right-angles to your board it will show you how much the starting line deviates from the right-angle. Now correct your board to a right-angle and you will see where the starting boat and mark 3 would have been.

The board is lying on the starting line, bow and stern in line with the buoys. If the sail flutters at right angles to the board, the starting line must be at right angles to the wind (below left)

The board is again lying on the starting line, but in this case bow and stern are not in line with the buoys. The angle at which the starting line deviates from the right angle to the wind can clearly be seen (below right)

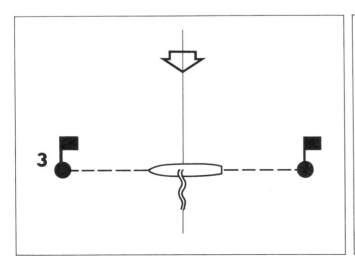

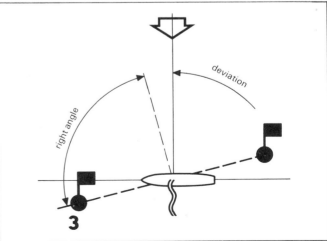

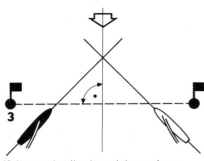

If the starting line is at right-angles to the wind, start on a port tack since you will have right of way

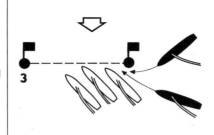

Remember the rule: lee before windward. The two black boards have no chance

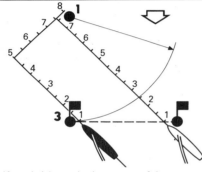

If mark 1 is not in the centre of the starting line the distances to the starting marks will be different

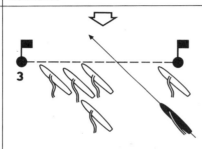

While the white boards are waiting at the starting line with sails fluttering, the black board is making full use of its distance and will be able to cross the line at full speed after the starting gun

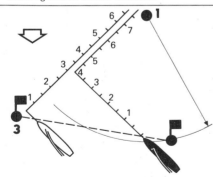

If mark 1 is not in the centre of the starting line, which itself is not at right-angles to the wind, the difference in the distances between the marks can be cancelled out

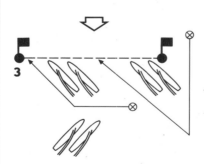

Keeping yourself in a good position with an eye on your watch saves you having to wait at the starting line

Before the Start

Look at your opponents. Where are most of them gathered? Where is there a gap?

Basic Rules:

1. Do not approach the line too early to avoid being driven over it.
2. Always, under all circumstances, keep yourself clear of other windsurfers. Start a little behind the others rather than get caught up in the crush.
3. Do not follow someone else. Calculate your own route from the starting line.
4. Put your watch right and then use it to prepare yourself for the starting gun.
5. It is better to take up a position in a gap in the second row and sail over the line with sail pulled in than to wait on the starting line and then be unable to get underway in the crush.
6. As soon as you have crossed the line take your bearings and go about in plenty of time. Do not stay in the shadow of the leaders.
7. After a successful start, concentrate on sail, course and technique. A windsurfing race is almost always decided at the start. In ninety per cent of cases the windsurfer who gets off to the best start wins.

The Race

All international windsurfing races are carried out on an 'Olympic Course'. The marks lie on the curve of a circle, in a triangular formation so that the course includes beating, reaching and running. The marks are always put into position just before the start of the race so that the officials can place the first mark exactly against the wind. As we can see in the diagram top left on p. 108, the starting line should be at right-angles to the direction of the wind. The course can be sailed clockwise or anti-clockwise:

- A red flag means clockwise (all marks remaining to starboard)
- A green flag means anti-clockwise (all marks remaining to port)

The complete course is: Start–1–2–3–1–3–finish

Distance to Mark 1

The diagram centre left on p. 108 shows a starting line which is positioned at right-angles to the wind. The first mark is not, however, lying in the centre of the starting line. It would be easy to conclude therefore that the best starting position is at mark 3 since this is nearer to mark 1. However, as we can see by the measurements, both boards have to sail the same distance to reach mark 1, but the white board has the advantage since it will arrive there on a port tack.

The deciding factor is not the distance between two marks, but how close to the wind the board is at the start. Another example will clarify the point – see the diagram bottom left on p. 108. Although mark 3 is farther from mark 1 than the second starting marker, the white boat will reach mark 1 earlier since mark 3 is closer to the wind.

Which Side of the Starting Line?

If the starting line is not at
right-angles to the direction of the
wind there is always a better side.
Normally you will get underway
with right of way on a port tack. In
the diagram at the top of this page
you can see, however, that a board
on a starboard tack, although it
does not have right of way, can get
a good lead over the 'port starters',
if it can make a good start. Of
course, a starboard start is always
risky since there is the danger of
coming into conflict with boards
having the right of way.

The Beat

The wheat is separated from the
chaff on this course and those who
have thundered up and down on a
broad reach the whole year
without practising their
close-hauled technique now
become apparent! The problem is
of finding a compromise between
standing still and as good a
forward thrust as possible. In light
breezes it is worth pointing higher.
The stronger the wind, the more
you should 'let your board run', not
least because the expenditure of
energy when sailing close to the
wind is enormous. Strong wind
causes waves and you will
therefore also have to contend
with being pushed from

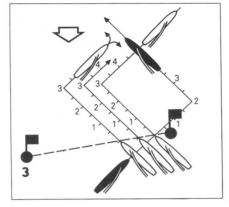

Sometimes it is worth starting on a
starboard tack so that on your next
manoeuvre you will have right of way

your course. Before the race
observe the waves, see which
direction they are coming from and
decide on which tack you will be
least affected by them. If you want
to calculate this more precisely
you must also determine in which
direction you will be shifted by the
current. From the result of these
observations you plan your tactics
for the beat. Do not forget that the
last stroke of the beat should be
from starboard to port, or you will
be rounding mark 1 without right
of way. Your technique during the
beat should be carefully and slowly
carried out. Avoid any violent
movements. Everything is geared

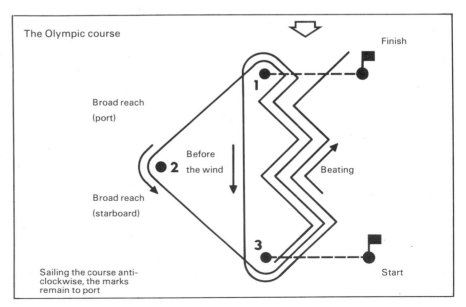

The Olympic course

Finish

1

Broad reach
(port)

Before
2 the wind

Beating

Broad reach
(starboard)

3

Start

Sailing the course anti-
clockwise, the marks
remain to port

In a changeable wind it is worth beating up to the mark using small tacks. If you use long tacks you risk the wind turning in an unfavourable direction

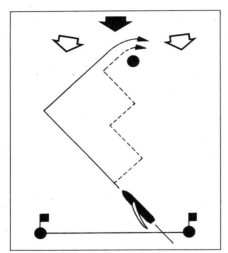

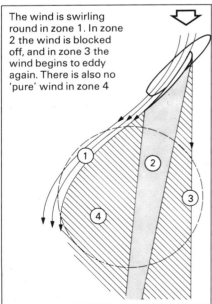

The wind is swirling round in zone 1. In zone 2 the wind is blocked off, and in zone 3 the wind begins to eddy again. There is also no 'pure' wind in zone 4

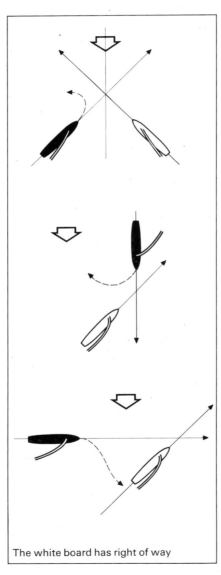

The white board has right of way

to gaining as much height as possible with every metre you move forwards. Constantly watch the gusts diagonally ahead to windward. Just before the wind drops, slacken the sail a little; as soon as the wind increases pull in and luff up, going carefully, however, and keeping the board constantly in motion, trying not to cut under the waves. Have a look at your opponents. Is anyone pointing higher than you? Is this because of your sail or your opponent's wind?

Rounding the Mark

As soon as you are coming up to the mark decide whether you are going to be able to round it easily or if you are going to be forced to go about again because you are blanketed by other boards. Never try rounding the mark if you are hemmed in; it is better to keep yourself free of the crowd and go ten metres beyond the mark than be 'mown down' in the crush.

Broad Reach – Speciality Course for Windsurfers

Here 'windsurfing' in the true sense of the term comes into its own. The bow must not lift too high out of the water. The stern must not sink too deep in the water. The whole length of the board must, if

possible, be kept on the water
(length means speed). Keep your
centre of gravity as close as
possible to the board. You will find
that you have to incline your mast
right over to windward, which
means that your board will cut
under when crossing the waves.
You will have to kneel or bend
down close to your board – you will
not be able to do it standing
upright. Your body would function
like a pendulum and the board
would cut under. Avoid the most
common mistake on the broad
reach course – pulling in your sail
too far. You should slacken off until
the sail is fluttering and then pull in
a hand's width – this will be your
best sail position.
It is on this course that
experienced surfers will start to

At the beginning of this race(wind force 5)
only a few windsurfers will manage to be on
the starting line at exactly the right moment

overtake. You are surfing just
behind and to windward of your
opponent until he has to slow
down because of your
downcurrent. You then bear away
towards him, accelerate, luff up
again and the resultant 'swing' will
take you in front. This is a crucial
manoeuvre when approaching
mark 2. Of course, you should have
made sure of your inside position
early so that you can round the
mark without having to battle for
your position. However, you can
also sometimes successfully luff
up from a position to leeward, and
get into the inside position from
behind your opponent.

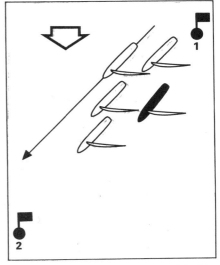

After having rounded mark 1 it is advisable
to stay on the outside, taking up your inside
position shortly before mark 2

113

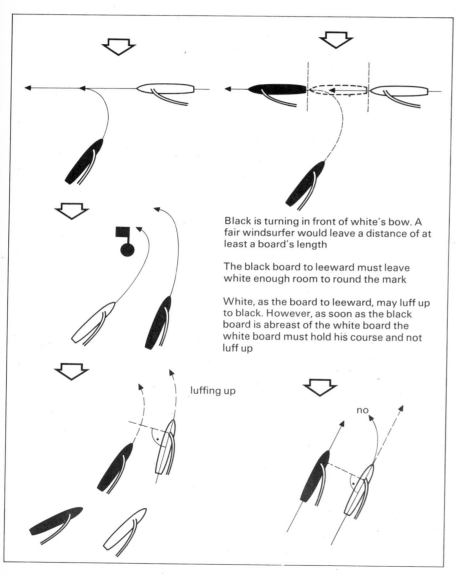

Black is turning in front of white's bow. A fair windsurfer would leave a distance of at least a board's length

The black board to leeward must leave white enough room to round the mark

White, as the board to leeward, may luff up to black. However, as soon as the black board is abreast of the white board the white board must hold his course and not luff up

luffing up

no

After rounding mark 2 you are still reaching but it is now closer to a beam reach than a broad reach. Remember not to pull in your sail too close. The second beat will be a lot easier: the field has opened up and you can concentrate on your tactics, provided you have paced yourself correctly. While beating do not forget to breathe in deeply, holding the oxygen in your lungs for a short time before breathing out completely. A correct breathing technique as used in yoga will help to relax and calm you. At the slightest sign of cramp change your tack immediately, using the going-about procedure to shake all your limbs. Change grips often (see p. 95) and do not forget to be searching constantly for the correct leg position. The more you use your body to balance and cushion the jolts, the less danger there is of capsizing. A capsize costs more dearly than any other fault. Therefore do not take risks; it is better to windsurf a little cautiously than to get left behind altogether if you capsize.

Before the Wind, the Most Difficult Course

Between mark 1 and mark 3 the technically expert windsurfer with his excellent legwork comes into his own. Keeping a running course in winds greater than Force 4 is in itself a masterly achievement when windsurfing normally, but in a race you must also maintain maximum speed! Therefore, never surf at right-angles to the waves but glide diagonally across them, i.e. beat down before the wind. Take a look at your opponents behind. Are they forming a wall and thus blocking your wind? Then there is nothing for it but to gybe and sail on a broad reach course out to the side of them. A word about leg position while running. If the wind is fresh and is making waves your legs should be well apart on the board, well away from the daggerboard case. Wherever possible kneel down so that your centre of gravity remains close to the board, thus avoiding being pushed forwards by the wind.

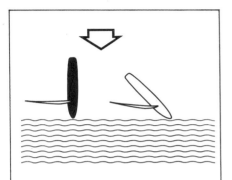

On a running course you should never sail at right-angles to the waves but cross them diagonally

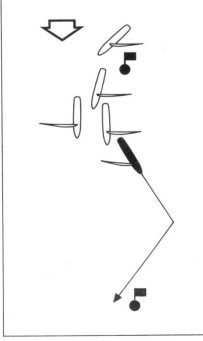

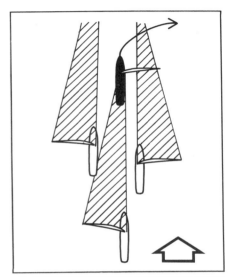

◀ As soon as a following boat takes the wind from your sail you should tack before the wind

On a running course you must constantly ▶ watch the boards behind you to avoid having all the wind taken out of your sail

The most important flags:

The Gybe: The Most Dangerous Manoeuvre

Prepare to round mark 3 in plenty of time. This is usually done by means of a gybe. Start early and shift your sail before you reach the mark, at the latest when you are at the side of it, then on a beam reach go past the mark and immediately luff up. By doing this you will often gain 50 m height. It is a bad mistake to wait until you are on top of the mark before beginning your rounding procedure since you will be 20 m past it before actually turning! When carrying out the gybe move the end of the boom close to the water and pull the sail in; never keep your mast upright. The board will describe a small circle only if the sail's centre of effort is moved right over to the side. You must also try, of course, to round mark 3 in the inside position.

And then on to the finishing line. The final beat will almost certainly go well. You have already sailed the course twice and you should make full use of wind variations and shore formations and any other characteristics which could be useful to you. Do not repeat mistakes made on the first beat. Find the end of the finishing line which is nearest to you. Is it the finish boat or the mark? Before the **last stroke of your beat make sure**

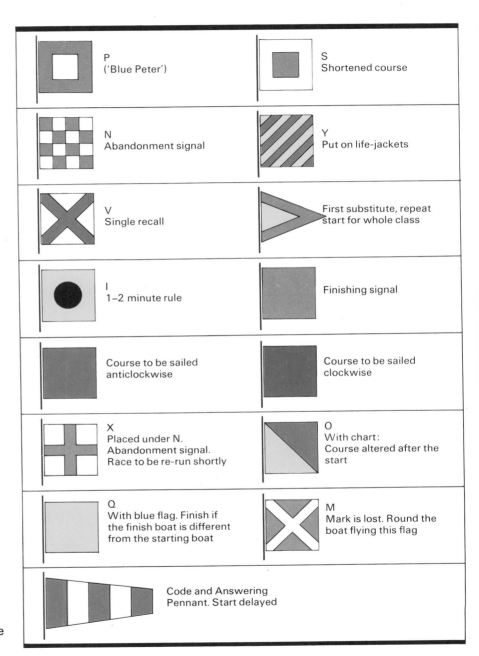

P ('Blue Peter')

S Shortened course

N Abandonment signal

Y Put on life-jackets

V Single recall

First substitute, repeat start for whole class

I 1–2 minute rule

Finishing signal

Course to be sailed anticlockwise

Course to be sailed clockwise

X Placed under N. Abandonment signal. Race to be re-run shortly

O With chart: Course altered after the start

Q With blue flag. Finish if the finish boat is different from the starting boat

M Mark is lost. Round the boat flying this flag

Code and Answering Pennant. Start delayed

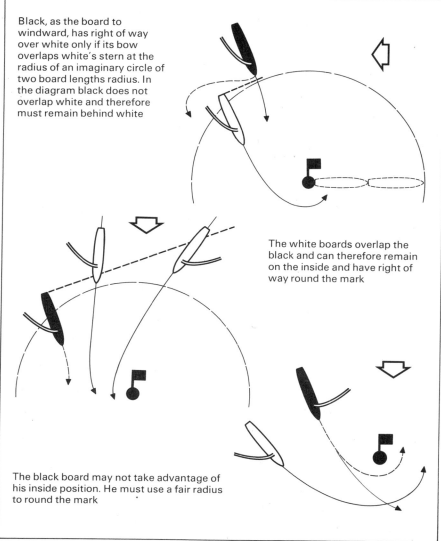

Black, as the board to windward, has right of way over white only if its bow overlaps white's stern at the radius of an imaginary circle of two board lengths radius. In the diagram black does not overlap white and therefore must remain behind white

The white boards overlap the black and can therefore remain on the inside and have right of way round the mark

The black board may not take advantage of his inside position. He must use a fair radius to round the mark

you have enough height. The mistake is often made of cutting the final stroke too fine so that you have to go about again, thus relinquishing your hard-earned place to opponents on a port tack. Always remember: in a hard-fought race fairness and good sportsmanship will always come out as winner. Particularly in races where you meet colleagues from other areas and countries, you should do everything in your power to see that the race does not end up in a battle of masts and booms! To take part is all that matters.

With a good lead, this windsurfer is shooting towards the finish

Tandem Windsurfing

Equipment

To stand with a partner on a board, to share the wind, go much faster and steer together – that is tandem windsurfing. The board is up to 8 m long with two rigs, one behind the other. The principle of steering is the same as for one-man windsurfing. On a tandem there is also a combined sail centre of effort which is taken from both sails and stands in a definite relationship to the centre of lateral resistance. While on a normal windsurfer to move the sail's centre of effort you have to incline the sail forwards, on a tandem it is enough to slacken one of the sails, leaving the other to do all the work. The result is that the sail's centre of effort is moved so that the board bears away or luffs up. This manoeuvre can be aided if the man who is steering inclines his sail as on a one-man windsurfer, i.e. when bearing away the bow-man inclines his sail forward while the stern-man slackens his sail. When

luffing up, the stern-man inclines his sail aft while the bow-man slackens his sail. Steering is therefore a joint effort.

A tandem board is ideally suited to teaching beginners. As it is very stable in the water and is difficult to tip over, a pupil can be taught the sailing technique and the use of the rig with an instructor actually on board. One rig only is used so that it is, in effect, a large one-man windsurfer.

Getting Underway

Basically, getting underway requires the same procedure as for a one-man board. Both men carry out the procedure together, the bow-man being careful not to pull in his sail too far so that the stern-man gets enough wind into his sail. It is a general rule that on a tandem the bow-man travels with a slacker sail while the stern-man can keep his sail very tight. It is a good idea for the lighter man to take up the stern position so that he can lean right out to windward, while in front the heavier man prevents the bow from lifting up and can also hold his sail while standing in an upright position. Because of the different positions of the masts, the stern sail avoids

the air turbulence caused by the bow sail.

Going About

The bow-man releases the boom and holds the rig by the mast rope while the stern-man pulls his sail in as normal, takes the boom towards the water and pulls it over. As soon as the bow has gone through the wind the bow-man starts the going-about manoeuvre and pulls the bow out of the wind into its new angle for getting underway. The stern-man now automatically goes about and gets underway. After going about the bow-man starts the procedure for getting underway so that the board turns a little farther out of the wind, the stern-man having an easier job since the board is already moving.

The Gybe

For the gybe the bow-man bears away while the stern-man lets his sail flutter. As soon as the bow approaches the wind direction the bow-man shifts his sail. Then the stern-man also changes the wind side, the bow-man keeping his sail slack while the stern-man luffs up.

A trapeze belt saves energy. If you can balance well you will even be able to take one hand off the boom

5

4

3

6

7

8

A tandem is steered in a similar fashion to a one-man board by changing the sail centre of effort and the centre of lateral resistance

To go about the bow sail is slackened and the stern sail pulled in. As soon as the board is pointing into the wind the bow-man is the first to move over to the new windward

side. He pulls his sail in and bears away by inclining his sail forward. The stern-man then also changes sides and adjusts his sail to match the bow sail

2

1

9

10

Before the Wind

On a running course with a tandem you can carry out the so-called butterfly technique, in which one man holds his sail to port and the other to starboard. With the sails in this position you will no longer be able to see whether the board is travelling on a starboard or port tack. If necessary you will have to come to an agreement beforehand about your sailing technique. A suggestion when butterfly windsurfing is that you sail with the stern sail (the bow sail therefore becoming a sort of foresail) so that the position of the stern sail determines the sailing direction.

Tandems have three mast foot slots so that the board can be used as a one-man board. If, for example, one of the windsurfers gets out of breath, the other can get it safely to the shore. The third slot can also be used for a third man. The three rigs will overlap each other but it is enormous fun to steer a tandem carrying about 18 square metres of sail. The positions of the sails from bow to stern are from slack to tightly pulled in; the bow-man keeps his sail slack while the centre-man can pull in a little. If the bow-man and centre-man pull in their sails too far very little wind would reach the stern sail and the third in line would be constantly in the water!

3

2

1

4

5

In strong winds the bow-man should go about very quickly. While the stern-man is still standing to leeward, the bow-man pulls the board out of the wind to its new position for getting underway

To go about the bow-man slackens his sail, while to gybe he pulls it in and inclines it forward
When you sail close to the wind a funnel effect between the sails is produced. When the butterfly technique is used on a running course, the stern sail determines the course

Tandem Technique

Steering a tandem is very easy if the crew work together. Especially when racing, one person should be the 'skipper' and be responsible for the sail positions, when the manoeuvres are to be made, etc. Normally the skipper will be the stern-man since he can see both sails and thus make sure of the best sail position. It is very difficult

to get close to the wind on a tandem. The trick is to press the windward edge of the board down, thus increasing the lateral surface. A few centimetres result in a considerably increased lateral surface which means that you can sail closer to the wind. You can also 'set the sails towards each other' by inclining the bow sail back a little and the stern sail forward a little. This results in a funnel effect between bow and

stern sails. In winds stronger than Force 6 you should always use storm sails.
Tandems are especially popular among racing windsurfers. Tandem racing, where the windsurfers share the struggle to win a race and complement each other's technique and tactics, is becoming more and more popular.

Specialist Windsurfing

Climbing the stern wave of the power-boat while holding on to the rope

Kneel on the board until the power-boat begins to pull the board

The wave is under the stern; you move your weight forwards

As soon as the board begins to move, stand up on one foot

Let go of the rope and surf on the stern wave of the boat

Before the boat starts to throw up high waves make sure you are standing on your board

Board Skiing

You can have great fun with a board without a rig, by board skiing, for example. To do this you hold on to a 30 in rope and are towed along by a motor boat, in a similar manner to a water skier.

However, remember the following:

You should cover up the hole in the daggerboard case or it will produce a metre-high fountain of water. You start off in a straight line behind the boat and then try to ski to the right and left over the waves, if you dare! To do this you stand to the left or right of the mast foot slot or a little behind it. The nearer the feet to the edge of the board, the safer your position will be. Before board skiing you must make sure that the skeg is firmly attached. Loose skegs will bend sideways and even break the board under the enormous strain. The board must also be free of cracks or holes in the daggerboard case. Cracks may not be apparent when windsurfing, but when you are skiing the enormous water pressure will mean that they can admit several litres of water in a very short time.

Windsurfing with a Trapeze

While you may smile at do-it-yourself experts who have constructed all sorts of hand holds, gloves with hooks and various gripping devices, there is an aid to strong windsurfing which is becoming more and more popular – the trapeze. When surfing with a trapeze you wear a special belt which is hooked directly on to the boom or on a rope which is fastened round the boom. There is an automatic hook available which releases itself from a safety line if you fall from the boom. Windsurfing with a trapeze means that you save energy and it is therefore recommended to all windsurfers who like to windsurf in strong winds.

By using a trapeze belt you can release your sail hand or mast hand completely

You use both hands for steering

As soon as you stand close to the boom, the trapeze hook releases the line

129

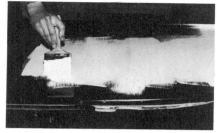
A thin layer of paint is applied to the shell, which has been waxed

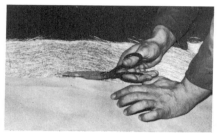
The matting is cut to the shape of the board

Building your own Windsurfer

To build your own windsurfer you will need a model. In our example we are using the Mistral-surfer. Two grp halves are prepared from the model. These thick halves are an exact copy of the upper surface and underwater surface of the model. Hans Taubinger, an engineer and a very experienced windsurfer, has been building his own boards since 1970, and uses the following method.

First of all both halves are waxed and covered with a dividing layer. Then a thin coloured layer is painted on to the two halves. After this has hardened (about forty minutes), the fibreglass matting (which has already been cut to shape) is laid in and soaked in polyester resin. The edges of the matting should be turned in so that

The liquid resin is poured directly on to the shell

The daggerboard case, skeg casing and standing area are strengthened

Clear plastic plates are screwed on to the halves

The resin is spread uniformly

All tools are immediately cleaned in acetone

Foam is poured into the tilted shell

later, when you stick the halves together, you have an edge inside the halves.

The mast foot, daggerboard case and fin areas and the whole standing surface are now strengthened with more fibreglass. When the matting has hardened for about one hour the whole thing is tilted about 30 degrees forwards so that the stern is in the air. Starting from below, clear plastic plates are screwed on to the edge.

The cold foam forms a curved dome which is cut off

The foam is levelled off with a simple saw

This is to prevent the foam which is going to be poured into the halves from running out. The two halves are now filled with foam, starting at the bottom and working up. As soon as both halves are filled, the extra foam is sawn off with a simple wood saw to bring the foam flush with the edges of the shells. You can finish off with a blade to make a fine surface.

The two parts are now stuck together. To do this, a thin layer of matting is laid on one half and soaked in resin. The halves are then stuck together and clamped. After the rough board has been smoothed down the daggerboard case, bow bumper, mast casing, skeg case, etc., are attached. Alternatively the two halves can be joined prior to foam filling and the liquid foam poured in through the stern a cupful at a time.

It takes two people about eighteen or twenty hours to complete a board, providing they have a complete model to work from.

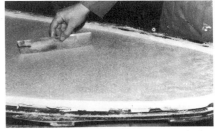

The surface of the foam is finished off with a blade

One half full of foam and finished off, ready to be stuck to the other half

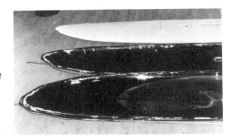

At the rear is the rough model, in the foreground the two halves

The slot into which the daggerboard case will later be fitted

Ice-sailing

Those who wish to carry on with their sport during the long winter months should try ice-sailing. Ice-sailors use a windsurfing rig but instead of the usual board it is fastened to a board about 1.5–2 m long, with three runners. You can reach speeds of up to 60 mph with this equipment. Ice-sailing is therefore one of the fastest wind-power sports.

The technique is similar to that of windsurfing. The mast foot sits in a slot just in front of the rear pair of runners. The front runner is either round so that it can slide sideways,

An ice-sailing board seen from below with its three runners. The front runner is either round or moveable

or moveable. If you move the sail's centre of effort backwards, the ice-sailing board will turn into the wind, and if you incline the sail forwards it will bear away. The whole thing is technically much easier than windsurfing, where you have to contend with the stability of the board and the waves. Ice-sailing boards are stable and are so wide that it is easy to walk round them. If there is enough wind you can even sit down. You can build your own ice-sailing board very cheaply. The most complicated part is the rig, which you will already have. All you need to do is build yourself a board and screw three runners on to it.

Ice-sailing boards reach very high speeds. The ice-sailer crouches down so that he does not have very far to fall!

Hot-Dogging

Windsurfing has something to offer everyone. It can mean so many different things to different people: a source of simple family fun, a deep experience of nature, a hard-fought race, the fun of stunt windsurfing. The tendency we can see in other sports, for example skiing, to leave behind the strict rules and regulations of the sport and enjoy it for its own sake, making it into a kind of game full of stunts and sometimes bordering on the lunatic, has entered windsurfing relatively early in its life. Only a few years after the introduction of the sport thousands of enthusiasts were windsurfing hot-dog style. Anyone can master this form of the sport since it is all about discovering new stunts for yourself and trying out new techniques on your board. To whet your appetite we will describe here some stunts popular among the windsurfers of Hawaii who, like all windsurfers in America, prefer freestyle surfing. In the USA there are already a great many competitions being held where the object is not to complete a set course in the shortest possible time but to demonstrate your skills and technique in front of a panel of judges. This variation of the sport is certain to catch on elsewhere and eventually become just as popular as racing.

Windsurfing on the Edge of your Board

If the mast foot tends to come away easily from your board you should wrap sticky tape round it so that it is firmly held in place. Take a beam reach course (wind no stronger than Force 4). Press your board to leeward with your front foot and grip the windward edge of the board with the toes of your rear foot. You should be able to stay in this position for a short time. When you can confidently do this balancing act, increase the pressure with the foot to leeward and pull the windward edge of the board up with the toes of the rear foot. At the same time bend your rear foot and kneel on the edge of the board. Then, very carefully, place your front foot on the edge and stand up, or you can remain kneeling.

Another way of surfing on the edge of your board is to raise the daggerboard halfway and use it as a kind of lever. Place your rear foot on the raised half of the daggerboard and when the board begins to tip over, place your other foot on the half of the daggerboard protruding underneath the board. If you do not manage to get both legs on the daggerboard extremely quickly you could injure yourself by falling on to the daggerboard.

Surfing to Leeward

In 1965 Newman Darby sailed the first steerable windsurfer on the lee-side. This means that the surfer, instead of standing on the windward side of the board, stands behind the sail to leeward and leans with the sail against the wind. In this position you can windsurf in winds up to Force 3 and even carry out manoeuvres like going about and gybing.

Windsurfing in the Boom

Surfing in the boom is an extremely sensible position which will save your energy and which has been practised in Europe for many years. Sailing on a beam reach with a slack sail, you slip under the boom and lean back on it against the wind. To begin with it is easier to hold the mast with the mast hand, laying the other arm along the boom. In this

135

position you use your whole body to bear away and luff up. To incline the sail forward you brace yourself with your rear foot, while to luff up you lean your whole body back. This technique is best suited to broad reach courses.

Turning Pirouettes

We have already learnt one way of turning the board 'on the spot' with the stop gybe. An even faster turn can be made by going about and then, during the luffing up phase, going as far aft as possible so that the bow swings through the wind in a single movement. You must then immediately move forward again and change over to the windward side by taking a single jump round the mast, or you will certainly fall in the water. You can execute a perfect pirouette if, after this very fast turn, you immediately do a stop gybe, i.e. land just on the windward side and, instead of getting underway, press the sail against the wind, turning the bow under the foot.

Windsurfing on the Bow or Stern

In order to be able to windsurf safely you need to get to know your board and all that it is capable of doing. While as a beginner you fell into the water if you went too close to the bow or stern, you should now, for fun, try to sail on a running course while actually standing on the bow or stern.
On a run the board can be braked by pulling it up. In this position you steer by means of a swing gybe since inclining the sail to leeward or to windward has little effect.

Pair Windsurfing

You surf very close to another windsurfer so that you can touch his board. The man to leeward now stands on the bow of the board to windward. This requires exceptionally good synchronisation of steering.

Butterfly Windsurfing

Both boards take a running course, one on a starboard and the other on a port tack. The gap is gradually closed until both boards are on a level. As soon as they touch each man places one leg on the other board. One man can even go through between the masts and stand in front of them, one foot on each board, as demonstrated by Karlheinz Stickl, twice West German windsurfing champion, in the photograph on p. 79.
These suggestions are merely meant to whet your appetite. There is no limit to the possibilities with your board. Whether you stand on the stern, surf on the edge of your board or try out new techniques with aids such as a trapeze, free-style windsurfing is an interesting and enjoyable variation of the sport.

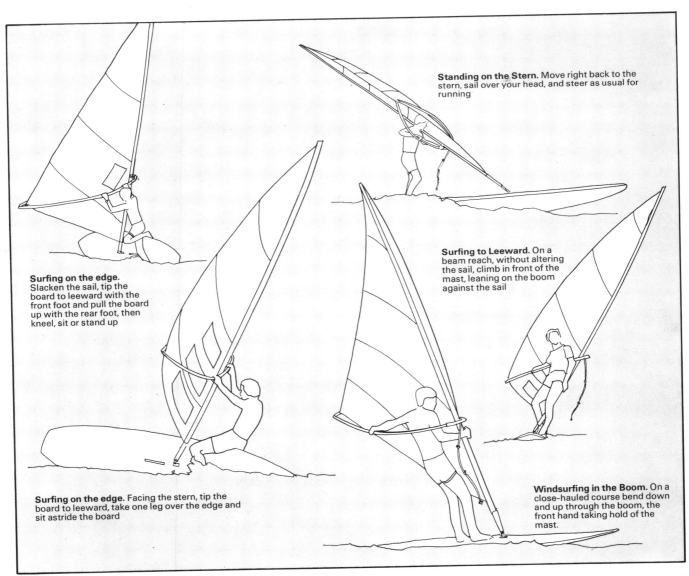

Standing on the Stern. Move right back to the stern, sail over your head, and steer as usual for running

Surfing on the edge. Slacken the sail, tip the board to leeward with the front foot and pull the board up with the rear foot, then kneel, sit or stand up

Surfing to Leeward. On a beam reach, without altering the sail, climb in front of the mast, leaning on the boom against the sail

Surfing on the edge. Facing the stern, tip the board to leeward, take one leg over the edge and sit astride the board

Windsurfing in the Boom. On a close-hauled course bend down and up through the boom, the front hand taking hold of the mast.

Windskating or Earth Surfing

A windsurfing rig can also be used as an extension to other sports, such as skateboarding. This sport, which originated in the USA, is increasing enormously in popularity. A do-it-yourself enthusiast will easily be able to construct a skateboard with a rig, by making a slot at the front of the board to take the mast foot. The skateboard is moved along by the strength of the wind and steered by you moving your weight around so that the moveable rollers can describe curves. Windskaters are recommended to wear knee and elbow pads and a crash helmet since the ground, unlike the water, is hard. Proper protective gear is readily available in shops; ice-hockey protective clothing is also suitable.

The Royal Yachting Association

The Royal Yachting Association is
the National Authority for the sport
of Board Sailing in the UK. A
training scheme has been set up,
which caters for the novice, those
who wish to become Instructors,
and the qualification of Trainers
who are qualified to teach both
novices and possible Instructors.
There are two booklets to go with
the scheme – G23, which contains
the syllabuses for the training
schemes; and G24, which is the
Instructor's Handbook, and these
are both available from the RYA.
The RYA has also drawn up a
Safety Code for Board Sailors,
again available from the RYA.

General information on where to
go to sail your board can be
obtained from the RYA, and we are
always pleased to hear your ideas
and suggestions.

JANE LAMBERT
Board Sailing Secretary

Class Associations

Sailboarding Association
Chairman, David Way,
28 Parkside, Wollaton,
Nottingham.
Telephone: 0602 25350

Windsurfer Class Association
Secretary, Tony Lee,
Brookmead, 7 Rudwicks Close,
Felpham, Bognor Regis,
Sussex.

Windglider Class Association
Goran Nyman,
Windsurfing Center UK
River Edge, Avoncliffe,
Alveston, Stratford on Avon.